hm
Learning and Study Skills Program
Level III

Developed by
The hm Study Skills Group

Author: Elaine M. Fitzpatrick

Senior Editor: David Marshak
Bureau of Study Counsel
Harvard University

Editors: Kiyo Morimoto, *Director*
Bureau of Study Counsel
Harvard University

Jerome A. Pieh, *Headmaster*
Milton Academy

James J. McGuinn

Rowman & Littlefield Education
Lanham • Boulder • New York • Toronto • Plymouth, UK

This title was originally published by ScarecrowEducation.
First Rowman & Littlefield Education edition 2007.

Published in the United States of America
by Rowman & Littlefield Education
A Division of Rowman & Littlefield Publishers, Inc.
A wholly owned subsidary of The Rowman & Littlefield Publishing Group, Inc.
4501 Forbes Boulevard, Suite 200, Lanham, Maryland 20706
www.rowmaneducation.com

Estover Road, Plymouth PL6 7PY, United Kingdom

Acknowledgments

Asimov, Isaac. *A Short History of Chemistry*. New York: Anchor Books, 1965, sentences, pp. 1, 6, 7, 23; paragraphs, pp. 25, 171.

Barrett, Shirley. "Causes of the Revolution," in *Exploring*, June 1976, p. 15.

Boston, July 1970, pic., p. 50.

Clough, Shepard B. et al. *European History in World Perspective: Early Modern Times*. Lexington, Mass.: D. C. Heath, 1975, pp. 686, 856–57, sentence, p. 717; paragraph, p. 567.

Churchill, Winston S. *Memoirs of the Second World War*. Boston: Houghton Mifflin, 1959, para. (modified), p. 276.

Dabagian, Jane. *Mirror of a Man*. Boston: Little Brown, 1975, sentences, pp. 101, 102, 104 (modified), 106, 143, 144, 203 (modified), ,354, 356, 360, 361, 366, 384.

DeMaria, Anthony. "Lasers," in *World Book Encyclopedia*, 1982, pp. 80a, 80b, 80c, abridged.

Heilbroner, Robert. *The Making of an Economic Society*. Englewood Cliffs, N.J.: Prentice-Hall, 1975, 80.

Henry, Alan P. "The Cradles of Civilization," in the *Boston Herald American*, August 27, 1981, p. 1.

Hilgard, Ernest R. et al. *Psychology*. New York: Harcourt Brace Jovanovich, 1975, pp. 248, 266–67, chap. 9 headings, para., p. 95.

Huberman, Leo. *Man's Worldly Goods*. New York: Monthly Review Press, 1936, para., pp. 5–6.

Hunt, E. K. *Property and Prophets*. New York: Harper & Row, 1975, para., p. 24.

Kane, Thomas S., and Leonard J. Peters. *Writing Prose: Techniques and Purposes*. New York: Oxford University Press, 1976, sentences, pp. 117 (modified), 236, 286, 335, 429.

Kirk, David. *Biology Today*. New York: Random House, 1975, sentences, pp. 267, 371, 787; paragraph, p. 42.

Lagemann, Robert T. *Physical Science: Origins and Principles*. Boston: Little Brown, 1967, para., p. 208.

Lobron, Carol. Excerpt from Review of John Hersey's *Aspects of the Presidency*, in the *Boston Globe*, August 24, 1980, p. A8.

Manning, David L. "Inflation, Education and the After-School Job," in *The Wall Street Journal*, March 11, 1980, p. 26.

Raloff, Janet. "Seeking Coherent Answers" (abridged) in *Science News*, September 18, 1981, pp. 184–85.

Shaffer, Richard. "The Big Picture," in *The Wall Street Journal*, March 5, 1980, p. 48 (abridged).

Student Learning Styles: Diagnosing and Prescribing Programs. Reston, Va.: National Association of Secondary School Principals, 1979, p. 42.

Tobias, Sheila. *Overcoming Math Anxiety*. New York: Houghton Mifflin, 1978, pp. 44–45.

"What Is the Third World?" in *U.S. News and World Report* (U.S. News and World Report, Inc.), March 31, 1975, p. 59.

ISBN: 978-0-8108-3804-8

TABLE OF CONTENTS

INTRODUCTION TO STUDY SKILLS

FROM HIGH SCHOOL TO COLLEGE

There's a difference between the high school class and the college course, usually quite a difference. In college, your classes will probably be a lot larger than they were in high school. Often you'll have professors who teach only through lecture. You'll have to spend a lot less time in the classroom, but you'll be expected to devote more time to learning on your own.

One way to make sense of these differences is to see them like this: to succeed in college, you have to be much more responsible for your own learning than you were in high school.

This book is designed to help you become more skillful at learning on your own. The study skills presented here are particularly useful for the kinds of learning most students need to do in college.

WHAT ARE STUDY SKILLS?

Study skills are *skills for learning.* These skills are efficient ways of learning in school and elsewhere.

When you learn study skills, you learn *how to learn* better.

Another way to understand study skills or learning skills is to see them as *problem solving methods.* Every course that you take in college will present you with a variety of learning "problems": for example, listening to a lecture and taking useful notes; working a problem set in math; reading a book and making sense of it; completing a science lab; and preparing for and taking an exam. Developing effective study skills and using them will help you to solve learning "problems" like these which you'll encounter in college.

Study skills are not a substitute for the work that learning requires. However, their use can make the effort and time you devote to learning more satisfying and rewarding.

HOW DO YOU LEARN STUDY SKILLS?

People learn study skills best by doing them, that is, practicing the skills. The activities in this book will introduce you to a wide range of effective study skills. You'll have the opportunity to try each of these skills, working with college level material.

To master a new study skill, you usually need to practice it at least three or four times or more. The more comfortable and automatic the skill feels to you, the more effective you'll be in using it.

When you first try a new study skill, it may feel uncomfortable or strange to you. Or, you may feel that the skill doesn't help you much. Both of these experiences are common. Whenever you start to learn a new skill, it's bound to feel unfamiliar. You may feel self conscious and awkward at first. This is quite natural. Usually it takes at least a few practices to become both comfortable with the skill and good at it. So when you start to work with a new study skill, don't give up after the first time if you feel uncomfortable or frustrated. Practice the skill at least a couple of times, and then see how well it works for you.

HOW DO YOU LEARN?

Imagine that you have just received a new bicycle that's not fully assembled. You have to install and adjust the brakes. You've never done this before. What would you do? (If you're a skilled bike mechanic, make up another example about which you know less.)

On the lines below, briefly describe how you'd go about *learning* to install and adjust the brakes on your new bike.

_____

_____

_____

_____

_____

_____

LEARNING STYLE

Not everyone learns in the same way. In fact, people learn in many different ways. For example, some people learn best when they can work with something new in a "hands-on" way. Others prefer to read about something new before they work with it. Still other people learn best when they can listen to new material. These examples are only a few of the ways in which people learn differently. There are many more.

The way or ways in which you learn best can be called your *learning style.* No ways of learning or learning styles are necessarily better than any others, but they are different.

What do you know about your own learning style? Right now, ask yourself, "How do I learn best?" Keep in mind that you may learn differently depending on what you're learning. Write your answers on the lines below. Use your own words. You may want to consider using some of the words listed below.

doing	learning from my mistakes	proving my point
working when I have to	reading	doing something I care about
experimenting	thinking about	being creative
writing	watching	talking it over
getting it right	listening	

"How do I learn best?"

_____

_____

_____

_____

_____

_____

MORE ABOUT LEARNING STYLE

Your learning style includes how you use your senses, how you think, and how you act. So it's not something simple. Rather, your learning style has many aspects or parts. You'll learn about two of these aspects below and about others as you work through this Program.

Perceptual preferences

Perception involves how you use your senses. While people use all of their senses as they learn, many or most individuals seem to learn best through one particular sense. What sense do you emphasize when you are learning best?

> *Auditory learners* learn best by hearing and listening.

> *Visual learners* learn best by seeing.

> *Kinesthetic* is a word which refers to sensation throughout your body, particularly in your muscles. *Kinesthetic learners* learn best through physical action: by doing, manipulating, and moving.

For example, to install and adjust the brakes on a bike, an *auditory* learner might talk with someone about how to solve the problem. A *visual* learner might start by reading carefully through the instructions and examining the diagrams and pictures included there. A *kinesthetic* learner might begin to work directly with the bike and brakes and only seek other resources to solve specific problems which come up.

Think about each of these perceptual styles. Do you recognize a part of your own learning style in any of them?

Groupings: Alone or with others

Some people learn best when they work alone. Others learn more effectively when they can discuss things with other people or work cooperatively. Some people like both styles but use them for different kinds of learning.

What style of grouping works best for you? Read the five styles below, and then rate them in terms of how you learn best. Put a #1 next to the style which works best for you, a #2 next to the style which works second best, and so on.

_____ By myself

_____ With a friend or two

_____ In a group of people

_____ With a tutor or teacher

_____ In different groupings for different kinds of learning

STUDY SKILLS AND LEARNING STYLE

Study skills are tools which you can use to help you learn. As with any tool, what's important is how well it works for you.

The concept of learning style explains that people learn best in their own personal ways.

What does learning style have to do with study skills? Think of it this way: you want to develop study skills that work for you as an individual learner; the more you know about how *you* learn best, the more you can use study skills which work well for you.

Each time you try a new study skill, first learn that skill just as it's taught to you. Once you know how to use the skill, ask yourself:

"How well does this study skill work for me?"

"In what ways can I improve how I use this skill? Is there any way I can make this skill more helpful?"

Try to find ways to make each new study skill more helpful to *you* as a learner. For starters, record here four elements about your learning style that you have identified in this introduction:

1. Perceptual preference _____

2. Grouping you prefer _____

3. _____

4. _____

UNIT I: LISTENING IS TUNING IN

LISTENING IS A SKILL

Many people think of listening as a natural ability, something to which they don't need to pay much attention. Yet most people are not good listeners. Just think for a few moments about how many times in the last few weeks you thought you were listening — and you weren't!

Hearing is a natural ability, a physical process. But listening is more than hearing. Listening means choosing to focus your attention on what you are hearing. It also means knowing what you've heard and trying to make sense of it.

Listening is a skill which requires your active participation. It's not just a matter of sitting back and relaxing. Even if you are an auditory learner, you need to listen skillfully if you want to learn well.

Listening is an active, meaning-seeking process. You listen so you can understand and learn.

Practice 1: Listen to the description which your instructor will read to you. As you listen, look at the diagram below and try to make sense of it.

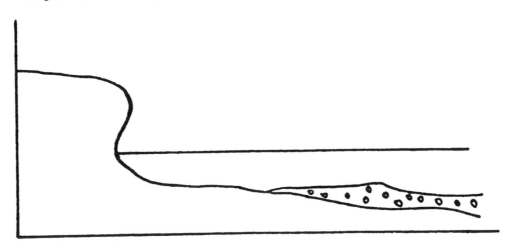

LEARNING TO TUNE IN

People usually talk at about 100-125 words per minute. However, we can think at a rate which is more than three times as fast, about 400 words per minute. Given this difference, it's not surprising that we often let our attention wander away from what someone is saying to us.

How can you keep your attention focused on what you are hearing?

The best way is to learn to tune in, to listen actively. A skillful and effective listener is an active listener.

ACTIVE LISTENING

Below you'll find five skills that you can learn to become more active as a listener. In the practices in this unit, you'll have the opportunity to try each of these skills.

Please note: These listening skills will be particularly useful to you for the kinds of listening you need to do in college.

1. *Choose to tune in to what you are hearing.*

   Consciously decide to listen. When you begin to listen, tell yourself: "I am awake and alert, and I'm choosing to listen carefully." Repeat this statement a few times with your inner voice when you start to listen or whenever you find your attention drifting away from the speaker. Or, make up a sentence of your own like the one above, and use it in a similar way.

2. *Try to figure out how the presentation you are hearing is organized. Then, use your understanding of that organization to guide your listening.*

   Often the speaker will give you organizational clues, i.e., a chalkboard or printed outline, a verbal summary, or a title. Clues like these can help you to find the main ideas and important details of a lecture or discussion.

   Ask yourself: What is the speaker telling me about how this presentation is organized? What organizational clues do I see or hear?

3. *When you need to remember what you are hearing, take notes about it.*

   Taking notes about a presentation will help you to learn the main ideas and important details. Take notes that make sense to you. When you take good notes, you can also use them later on when you write papers or study for exams.

   Ask yourself: Do I need to take notes about this presentation? What kind of notes will be most useful to me?

4. *While you listen, ask yourself questions about what the speaker is saying.*

   Remember: you can think three times as fast as the speaker can talk. Use your "extra time" to think about what she or he is saying. Try to make sense of the speaker's message.

   Ask yourself: What is the speaker telling me? What is she or he getting at? How is she or he supporting the points being made?

5. *Try to make a whole message of what you have heard. Then, evaluate it.*

   Take a few minutes at the end of the presentation for review. Go over the main ideas and important details which you have just heard. Try to make sense of them. Then, evaluate what the speaker has said. What do *you* think about these ideas?

   Ask yourself: What are the main ideas of the presentation? How do these ideas fit together? What do they mean? In what ways does what I've heard make sense to me?

Practice 2:   Your instructor will present a short lecture. Practice skills #1 and #2 above. At the end of the lecture, describe how the presentation was organized. Write your description on the lines below.

_____

_____

_____

_____

_____

PATTERNS OF ORGANIZATION

When you understand how a presentation is organized, you'll be better able to follow and make sense of it. Recognizing the pattern of organization will help you to understand what you're hearing. It will also allow you to take more organized notes.

A speaker may use several different patterns of organization in the same lecture. The more you can tune in to what patterns of organization he or she is using, the more effectively you can listen to what's being said.

Here is a list of common patterns of organization:

description or narration	definition
cause/effect	list
comparison/contrast	sequence/time

Practice 3: Below you'll find definitions for each of the six patterns of organization. On the lines under each definition, write the name of that pattern and a brief example of it.

Example

1. A series or group of ideas or facts; often in numerical order.

_____

_____

_____

_____

_____

_____

2. Explains the reasons for something or the effects of actions.

_____

_____

_____

_____

_____

_____

3. Indicates how two or more things are alike and/or how they are different.

_____

_____

_____

_____

_____

_____

4. Refers to the order in which events take place.

_____

_____

_____

_____

_____

_____

5. Tells about someone or something, often in great detail. Or, tells a story.

_____

_____

_____

_____

_____

_____

6. Explains the meaning of something.

_____

_____

_____

_____

_____

_____

Practice 4: Each sentence below is the first sentence in a lecture. Read each sentence, and write what you think will be the pattern of organization of that lecture on the line to the right. Then, underline the word(s) in the sentence which gave you the clue.

1. As we examine the performance of our schools, six basic truths — most of them a result of our mixing altruism and education — emerge time and again.   _____

2. What do we mean when we talk about the intensity of feeling?   _____

3. Though they shade into each other imperceptibly, it is useful for us to distinguish dictatorship from totalitarianism.   _____

4. So this is our topic for today: how does autokinetic motion occur?   _____

5. With the first light of dawn, Gregson watched the schooner ease into the shallows of the hidden cove.   _____

6. Let us trace the events which marked the decline and eventual dissolution of the Portuguese empire.   _____

7. Today we will look in detail at how the Mayas celebrated the coming of the new year.   _____

Practice 5: Your instructor will present a short lecture. Takes notes about this lecture in the space below. Use what you've learned about patterns of organization to help you.

Practice 6: Your instructor will present another short lecture. Practice skill #4 (on page 6) while you listen.

When the lecture is done, practice skill #5. In the space below, write the main idea(s) in the lecture. Then, evaluate this idea(s). Does it make sense to you? Why or why not? Write a few notes about your evaluation at the bottom of this page.

Main idea(s)

Evaluation

UNIT I SUMMARY: LISTENING IS TUNING IN

Listening means choosing to focus your attention on what you are hearing. It also means knowing what you've heard and trying to make sense of it.

Listening is an active, meaning-seeking process. A skillful and effective listener is an active listener.

You can become more active as a listener by using these five skills:

1. Choose to tune in to what you are hearing. Tell yourself "I'm awake and alert, and I'm choosing to listen carefully" when you begin to listen or when you find your attention drifting.

2. Try to figure out how the presentation you are hearing is organized. Then, use your understanding of that organization to guide your listening.

   Six common patterns of organization are: description or narration
   cause/effect
   comparison/contrast
   definition
   list
   sequence/time

3. When you need to remember what you are hearing, take notes about it.

4. While you listen, ask yourself questions about what the speaker is saying.

5. Try to make a whole message of what you have heard. Then, evaluate it.

LEARNING STUDY SKILLS ON YOUR OWN: I

At the end of each unit, you'll find a very short section called "Learning Study Skills On Your Own." Below you can see the first one.

Each of these sections will offer you ideas about learning and study skills which go beyond what can be covered in the units themselves. Some of these sections will extend the unit of which they are a part. Others will offer you new and useful ideas and suggestions about how people learn.

Each "Learning Study Skills On Your Own" gives you a starting point and a direction. It's up to you to follow through if you find value in it for your learning.

HOW DO YOU USE STUDY SKILLS?

Study skills are tools which you can use to help you learn. As with any other tool, what's important is how well they work for you.

When you approach a new study skill, first learn that skill just as it's taught to you. Then, once you know how to use the skill, ask yourself the questions below and answer them:

"How well does this study skill work for me?"

"Given my own learning style, are there ways that I can change this skill to make it more useful to me?"

Try to find ways to make new study skills more helpful to you as a learner. If a particular study skill doesn't work well for you, find one that does. If a study skill works fairly well, see if you can find ways to make it work better.

UNIT II: TAKING NOTES IS A COLLEGE SURVIVAL SKILL

WHY TAKE NOTES

One of the most important study skills you'll need to use in college is note taking. Taking notes about lectures, readings, and discussions is necessary if you wish to learn effectively and do well on exams. College instructors will usually hold you responsible for much more material than you were expected to know in high school. And the only way to stay on top of things is by taking notes about what you read and hear. For example, you can prepare for an exam much more readily by going over your notes than by trying to remember what you heard or read six weeks ago. You can also review much more effectively from notes than you can by trying to re-read all of your assignments.

When you take notes, you create a record of what you've heard or read. You also begin to make sense for yourself of what you are hearing or reading. You start to figure out what the main ideas and important details are and how this information relates to what you already know.

HOW TO TAKE NOTES

There are many good methods for note taking. Taking notes will be easier and more helpful to you when you use methods which fit your learning style. In one way, however, all of the methods are similar. Each one is designed to help you create a record of the main ideas and important details and examples in a presentation. When you take notes, remember that you don't need to write down everything that you hear or read. You only need the main ideas and important details.

This unit will involve you in working with several different note taking methods. Try each of them, and see which one(s) works best for you.

OUTLINING

Outlining is one effective way of taking notes. Outlines help you see the organization of the major and minor topics in a text, lecture, or discussion.

Look at page 13, and you'll see an outline form for the passage at the top of the page. Note that the *title* is written above the outline. The *main topics* or *main ideas* are marked with a Roman numeral and placed furthest to the left. *Sub-topics* or *secondary ideas* are indented slightly and marked with a capital letter. *Details* are indented still further and are marked with regular numbers.

Practice 1: Read the passage "Changing Trade Patterns." Then, complete the outline notes below the passage.

CHANGING TRADE PATTERNS

Late medieval and early Renaissance trade patterns may be represented by three interlocking circles. On the east was the great complex of Asiatic trade, touched at points on its western perimeter by Italian merchants. In the center was the circle of Mediterranean trade dominated by Venetians and Genoese but participated in by other Italians and by Spaniards, Portuguese, Netherlanders, and Frenchmen. On the northwest was the circle of Baltic trade with English commerce as a part. The circles overlapped in the Netherlands, particularly at such Flemish ports as Bruges, and in the ports of the Near East.

From the European point of view, the Mediterranean was central to this world trade pattern. A great share of European interregional trade passed at one time or another through the hands of merchants in Genoa, Venice, Barcelona, and Marseilles, or was carried through the Mediterranean area. The most important banking houses were located either in Italy or in south Germany and southeastern France on the overland trade routes from the Mediterranean region into the rest of Europe.

Trade Patterns in the Late
Middle Ages and Early Renaissance

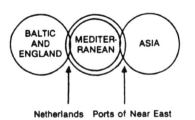

CHANGING TRADE PATTERNS

I. Late medieval and early Renaissance trade patterns

   A. Asiatic

   B. _____

   C. _____

   D. Overlap areas

      1. _____

      2. _____

II. _____, center to world trade

   A. Interregional trade

   B. _____

USING A DIAGRAM

Another way of taking notes is making a diagram. A diagram is really a picture of information. In taking diagram notes, you use the shape of the diagram to show how ideas and details relate to each other. Rather than using numbers and letters to organize the information as you did in an outline, you use lines, circles, squares, and so on. For example, the diagram below shows notes for the "Introduction To Study Skills" on page 1.

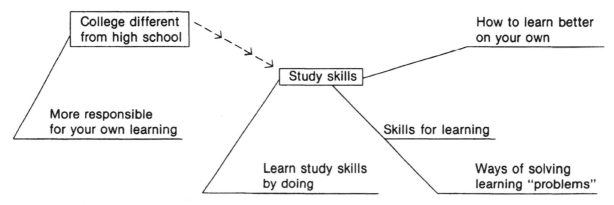

Sometimes you can find the shape of a useful diagram in your instructor's notes on the board or in an illustration in your book. When you use one of these sources for the shape of your diagram, you'll probably need to add information to it to create good notes.

Practice 2: Look at the illustration next to "Changing Trade Patterns" on page 12. Using this illustration as the shape of your notes, take diagram notes for this passage in the space below.

Mapping

One specific way of taking diagram notes is *mapping.* This method involves organizing your notes in such a way that they look like a map on your paper.

As you read the instructions for mapping below, look at the mapping notes for "Changing Trade Patterns" at the bottom of the page.

1. Write the *main topic* or *main idea* in the center of your page. Draw an oval or circle around it. (If there is more than one main topic or main idea, use more than one oval.)

2. Write the *sub-topics* or *secondary ideas* on lines connected to the oval around the main topic.

3. Write the *details* on lines connected to the *sub-topics* to which they are related.

4. Write the *title* at the top of the map.

   NOTE: With longer texts, lectures, or discussions, you will probably have more than one main topic. In that situation, circle the main idea of the entire passage, lecture, or discussion twice to show its importance.

CHANGING TRADE PATTERNS

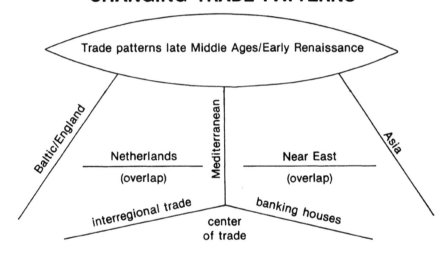

Practice 3: Read the passage below. Then, taking mapping notes for this reading in the form on page 15.

THE HISTORICAL SOURCES Some historians have believed that the annals of the poor do not exist. The history of European civilization, as they see it, is based on the written word. In the early modern world, and throughout the eighteenth century (under consideration in this section) eighty to ninety percent of the population consisted of peasants. Even in the most progressive of western European areas very few peasants could read or write and, therefore, tended not to leave written accounts of their activities. Further, some members of the upper and literate classes simply took the peasantry for granted, paying less attention to them than they did to their horses or their dogs. In short, the "common man" of early modern Europe has been supposed to have had no history.

Fairly recently, however, these negative attitudes toward the history of lower classes have been eroded as social historians have moved to the forefront of the profession and have begun to use all sorts of new materials and methods to study early modern society in all its aspects. As a result, the previously neglected humble people are now finding themselves posthumously reconstructed, counted, analyzed, and run through computers, as we move toward "total History."

Some of our sources for social history derive not from written records but from pictures. Occasionally we may receive marvelous visual flashes of peasant life through paintings like those by Pieter Brueghel the Elder (late sixteenth century) and Louis Le Nain (early seventeenth century) or of the urban poor through the paintings and engravings of William Hogarth (mid-eighteenth century). At least one contemporary French social historian (Philippe Aries) has imaginatively used artworks as historical sources (iconography) to trace the evolution of the nuclear family and changing attitudes toward children in early modern times.

Other, more nearly conventional sources of historical information about the submerged sectors of humanity are the records of those within the literate world who, though they had very little interest in how peasants lived and loved, were intensely interested — for economic reasons — in the fact of the peasants' existence. The landlord, insofar as he (or his bailiffs) could read, write, and cipher, kept records of his relationships with the peasant as they pertained to rents or dues owed. Large numbers of these estate (or manorial) records still exist in local repositories, and more and more they are being studied by social historians.

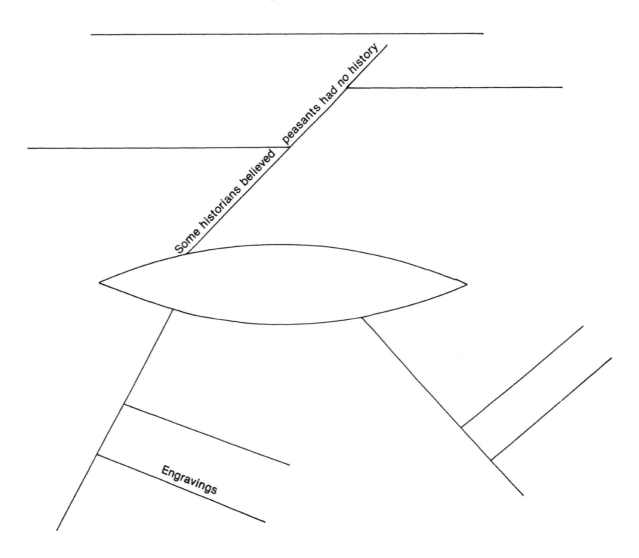

Using A Summary

A summary is a brief version of the original reading, lecture, or discussion. Like an outline, map, or diagram, a summary includes a title, the main ideas, the secondary ideas, and the important details.

Write your summary in a way which makes sense to you now and which will be clear to you when you come back to the summary in a few days, weeks, or months. *Use your own words,* except for technical terms and quotes. Write a summary in sentences and paragraphs.

Practice 4: On the lines below write a summary of the passage on pages 14 and 15. Limit your summary to 75 words or less.

_____

_____

_____

_____

_____

_____

_____

FINDING YOUR OWN STYLE

Now you've experimented with four different ways of taking notes. Each of these methods can work to provide you with useful notes.

You may have found one or two of these techniques more comfortable and helpful than the others. Think about your preferences for a moment, and then circle the one or two methods below which you liked the best.

outline

diagram

map

summary

THINKING ABOUT NOTE TAKING STYLE

You may already have a way of taking notes which is like one of these methods but somewhat different. That's fine. What's important is how well your note taking method works for you. If it works, then it's a good method. If it doesn't, then you need to change it.

You may want to learn all four of these methods and use them in different ways. For example, in taking notes from a book where the material is highly organized, you may choose outlining. In a discussion, the material is usually less organized, and you may find mapping to be a more effective method for you. Also, think about this: when you use mapping, you can start to take notes without knowing how everything fits together. Write down the ideas and information which seem important to you as you go along. Then, whenever you're ready, you can draw the "map."

During the next few weeks, experiment with how you take notes. See if you can discover which methods work best for you in which situations.

16

LISTENING AND TAKING NOTES

In many colleges, a high percentage of the classes are lectures. It's not unusual for freshmen to have three or four lecture classes because so many of the introductory courses are taught in this way.

The key to learning from a lecture is listening actively and taking useful notes. You can see one value of note taking in the anecdote below:

> It's the night before the first mid-term exam in the Introductory Psychology course. Without any lecture notes, Gail is frantically trying to re-read all of the hundreds of pages of reading assigned during the first six weeks of the semester. In contrast, Beverly is carefully going over her lecture notes, paying special attention to the ideas and concepts which her instructor said were particularly important. Later on she'll do the same with her notes from the readings.

When you take notes from a lecture, write down only what you need to include to construct a record of that presentation. Use your own words, except for technical terms and definitions. Remember: your notes are for you! Don't worry about writing sentences: write phrases, key words, and so on. If it helps you, draw diagrams and pictures.

At the end of the lecture, take a minute or two to look over your notes. Ask yourself: "What are the main ideas here? Does this make sense to me? What have I learned about this?" Write down any other words you need to complete your notes. You can also include any ideas, comments, or questions that occur to you!

Practice 5: Your teacher will deliver a short lecture. Use one of the methods introduced in this unit or your own method to take notes. Write your notes below.

Before you begin, look over the summary of listening skills on page 11. Use as many of these skills as you can while you listen.

_____

_____

_____

_____

_____

_____

_____

_____

_____

_____

_____

_____

17

UNIT II SUMMARY: TAKING NOTES IS A COLLEGE SURVIVAL SKILL

Note taking is one of the most important study skills you'll need to learn in college. When you take notes, you begin to make sense of what you're hearing or reading. Also, your notes are very helpful when you prepare for an exam or test.

There are many effective ways of taking notes. Four of these methods are:

1. **Outlining**	Write the title above the outline. The main ideas are marked with a Roman numeral and placed farthest to the left. The secondary ideas or sub-topics are indented slightly and marked with a capital letter. Details are indented still further and are marked with regular numbers.
2. **Using a diagram**	Use lines, circles, squares, and so on to organize information into a diagram or "picture."
3. **Mapping**	Write the main idea in the center of your page. Draw an oval around it. Write the sub-topics or secondary ideas on lines connected to the oval around the main topic. Write the details on lines connected to the sub-topics to which they are related. Write a title at the top of the map.
4. **Using a summary**	A summary is a brief version of the original reading, discussion, or lecture. Write a summary in sentences and paragraphs. Use your own words, except for technical terms and quotes.

What's most important in choosing a note taking method(s) is how well it works for you. You may want to learn several ways of taking notes and use different methods in different kinds of learning situations.

LEARNING STUDY SKILLS ON YOUR OWN: II

What Else Can You Do With Mapping?

Each of the note taking skills included in this unit can be very effective. However, mapping offers some particular values which result from the way maps are created.

Have you ever tried to start an outline in the middle? If you have, you know how difficult it is. With outlining and other sequential note taking methods, you really have to start at the beginning. That means that you have to know how the ideas and information are organized before you can begin to take notes.

When you are mapping, you can start anywhere. When you don't know where the beginning is, just jot down the important ideas and information on your paper as you go along. Then, you can draw the lines connecting them into a map whenever you learn what the connections are.

Mapping can be an emergent method of taking notes rather than a sequential one. This means that you can discover the organization of ideas and information as they emerge while you read, watch, listen, or think.

If you're interested in learning more about mapping, look at Tony Buzan's *Using Both Sides of Your Brain,* pages 83–106 (New York: E. P. Dutton and Co., 1974).

Can you see clear pictures or images in your mind's eye? Some people can, and some can't. (You can learn to see mental pictures or images more clearly by practicing.) If you can see mental images, you can study your mapping notes by visualizing the notes, that is, seeing a mental picture of your mapping notes. Visualize the map clearly and study the image for at least a few seconds. Then, you'll probably be able to recall your mental picture of the map when you want to do so. Experiment with this, and see how well it works for you.

UNIT III: LEARNING TO SURVEY

WHAT IS SURVEYING?

One useful skill which can help you learn from your reading more effectively is *surveying*. When you survey, you look quickly through the reading material to gain a sense of the organization and gist of what you will later read more carefully.

Surveying takes only a few minutes and gives you a sense of focus and direction in your reading. Also, since you go over the main ideas in the material when you survey, you begin to learn about them. You'll probably be surprised at how much you can learn just from surveying. In Practices 1 and 2, you'll have an opportunity to see.

SURVEYING A CHAPTER

There are different kinds of surveys. Just as the way you read will vary according to your purpose for reading, so will the kind of survey you conduct.

One kind of survey is for material which you need to cover in detail, for example, a chapter in a textbook or an article from a magazine. In a *chapter survey*, there are four basic steps:

1. Read the *title* and ask yourself what it means.

2. Read the *introduction* to find out what the chapter is about.

3. Read the *chapter headings* and *sub-headings.* Try to phrase each one as a question which could be answered by a careful reading of the section beneath it.

4. Read the *chapter summary.* Then, tell yourself what the chapter is about as if you were explaining it to a friend. (When you explain something to another person, it helps you to understand it better.)

When you survey a chapter or article, you learn about the skeleton of ideas in your reading. Then, you need to read the chapter or article carefully to flesh out that skeleton.

Practice 1: On pages 21–22, you will find the title, introduction, chapter headings and sub-headings, and summary of a chapter from a college psychology textbook. Note that you will have only the "skeleton" for the chapter, not the chapter as a whole.

Answer each of the underlined questions below by referring to the material on pages 21–22. In doing this, you will follow the steps of a chapter survey.

You may not be able to answer all of the questions. You may use a dictionary to help you.

What does the title of this chapter mean?

_____

_____

_____

According to the introduction, with what four major issues will this chapter be concerned?

1. _____
   _____

2. _____
   _____

3. _____
   _____

4. _____
   _____

Answer the four questions below by referring to the headings and sub-headings of the chapter listed on page 21.

1. What is CAI?

   _____

2. In what ways might reward help and/or hinder your (or anyone else's) learning?

   _____
   _____
   _____

3. In what ways might punishment help and/or hinder your (or anyone else's) learning?

   _____
   _____
   _____

4. Find a topic on page 21 that you'd like to learn more about and explain why.
   Topic:_____
   Why? _____
   _____

Read the chapter summary. Now write two questions of your own about material in the summary which is not clear to you.

1. _____
   _____

2. _____
   _____

CHAPTER "SKELETON"

TITLE   **Chapter 9 Optimizing Learning**

INTRODUCTION

Most research on learning and memory suggests practical applications, but it is seldom possible to move directly from research to applications. Usually it is necessary to take account of the setting, to try out the research findings in practical contexts, and adjust for special conditions. A drug may be found to kill the bacteria causing a given disease, but before this knowledge can be put to use, the proper dosage and method of administration must be determined and possible side effects evaluated. In this chapter we examine some laboratory findings that bear upon problems of efficient learning and yield suggestions for optimizing the learning process. We will be concerned with such issues as the structure of an individual's knowledge base and how best to add to it, the way in which learning one set of materials transfers to learning another, the importance of immediate information feedback, and motivational and emotional factors that affect learning efficiency.

Much of society's energy is devoted to the management of learning — to instruction in schools, to job training in industry, and to teaching health and safety procedures in the community. The aim of an applied psychology of learning is to produce the highest quality learning with the greatest possible efficiency. In recent years there have been many public discussions about which teaching methods are most effective; particular emphasis has been placed on the teaching of basic skills like reading and mathematics. All these discussions concern the appropriate applications of the principles of learning to the field of instruction.

A number of teaching aids have been developed to promote learning. Motion pictures, audio-visual tapes, and closed-circuit TV have become important adjuncts to instruction. Relative newcomers on the instruction scene are programmed texts and computer-assisted instruction. Although still in the developmental stage, such work is worth considering because of the way in which it illustrates learning principles.

HEADINGS
AND
SUB-HEADINGS

PROGRAMMED LEARNING AND AUTOMATED INSTRUCTION

    Computer-Assisted Instruction
    Instructional Programs
    Effective Teaching Procedures

        1. Active participation
        2. Information feedback
        3. Individualization of instruction

TRANSFER OF LEARNING

    Doctrine of Formal Discipline
    Learning to Learn
    Transfer by Mastering Principles
    Application to Education

IMAGERY AS AN AID TO LEARNING

REWARD AND PUNISHMENT IN THE CONTROL OF LEARNING

    Intrinsic and Extrinsic Rewards
    Controlling Learning Through Punishment

       PROS AND CONS ON THE USE OF PUNISHMENT

ANXIETY AND LEARNING

    Anxiety and Competing Responses
    Anxiety and Academic Performance

SUMMARY

1. *Computer-assisted instruction* (CAI) is proving to be a valuable aid to learning. Instructional programs designed for CAI may be in the form of *linear programs,* in which the student progresses along a single track from one frame to the next, or *branching programs,* in which the material to be presented next depends upon the student's response to previous frames. When a linear program is presented in book form it is called a *programmed text.*

2. Some of the features of programmed instruction and CAI that make them effective are: active participation by the learner, immediate feedback, and rate and path through the learning materials adjusted to individual differences.

3. The influence that learning one task has on the subsequent learning of another task is called *transfer of learning. Positive transfer* occurs when one task facilitates the learning of another; when there is interference we have *negative transfer.*

4. Factors that produce positive transfer include *learning to learn* (learning to relax in the situation, to ignore irrelevant stimuli, and to distinguish the relevant cues) and learning general *principles.*

5. In classroom situations transfer occurs best when there is a clearly designed effort on the teacher's part to emphasize similarities between the current subject and the situation to which the new learning will transfer, and to stress the application of principles.

6. In attempting to guide the learning of another person, *reward* is generally favored over *punishment.* Reward strengthens the rewarded behavior, whereas punishment may not lead to unlearning of the punished behavior; instead, the behavior may be merely suppressed, reappearing again when the threat of punishment is removed or perhaps appearing in disguised form.

7. Punishment may be effective, however, when it forces the individual to select an alternative response that can then be rewarded, or when it serves as an *informative cue* to avoid a certain response. Arbitrary rewards and punishments have some unfavorable consequences, in part because of the authoritarian control they often imply.

8. Subtle *emotional factors,* based on personal experiences of the individual, play a central role in learning. When college students are separated into *high-anxious* and *low-anxious* groups, the high-anxious subjects often perform better than the low-anxious ones in simple conditioning situations, but they do less well on complex tasks. Pressure on high-anxious students to do better may actually impede their performance, while such pressure spurs the low-anxious students to improve. High anxiety is also significantly related to lowered grade-point averages and dropout rates among college students.

MORE ABOUT CHAPTER SURVEYS

You may want to add two other steps to your survey when these are appropriate:

1. Look at all the visuals in the chapter or article: the graphs, maps, pictures, illustrations, etc. Often these are used to illustrate main ideas.

2. When your instructor comments about a reading assignment when she or he assigns it, pay careful attention. Then, relate these comments to your survey. Often your instructor will tell you what he or she thinks is important in a reading.

Surveying a chapter can also help you to anticipate quiz or test questions. When you find important ideas or information in a survey, you have located a potential source of quiz questions.

Remember: the purpose of surveying is not to avoid reading the chapter or article. Rather, the survey works to provide you with (1) some initial learning about the reading and with (2) a framework which will help you to learn more when you read the chapter carefully.

Practice 2: Your instructor will ask you to survey a chapter in one of your textbooks. You will have only *six* minutes for the survey. Then, your instructor will give you a short "quiz" about the chapter. See how well you do!

SURVEYING A BOOK

Another kind of survey is useful when you expect to read all or most of a book. You can do a *book survey* to discover the following:

1. What is this book about?

2. What parts does this book have that will make it easier to understand?

In Practice 3, you'll go through the steps of a book survey and see how they work.

Practice 3: Answer each of the questions below.

What is the TITLE of the book?

_____

From the title, what do you think the book is about?

_____

Who is the AUTHOR(S)? _____

What is the DATE OF PUBLICATION?_____

What can you learn about this book from the INTRODUCTION AND/OR PREFACE? Read the introduction and/or preface; then write one or two sentences which summarize them.

_____

_____

_____

_____

What can you learn about this book from the TABLE OF CONTENTS? Look at the table of contents, and write one idea or understanding that you've gained from it.

_____

_____

Does this book include an INDEX? _____ A GLOSSARY? _____

An APPENDIX? _____

Do the chapters have INTRODUCTIONS AND/OR SUMMARIES? _____

What are the two most useful learnings you've gained about this book from the survey you have just conducted?

1. _____

_____

2. _____

_____

READING WITH PURPOSE

Effective readers set purposes of their own. And they learn from their reading more efficiently.

You can use your survey to set a purpose for your reading. For example, after you've surveyed a chapter or book, ask yourself:

What do I want and/or need to learn from this reading?

What in this reading most interests me?

Answer these questions or ones like them, and then read the material with your purpose(s) in mind.

UNIT III SUMMARY: LEARNING TO SURVEY

One of the most useful study skills that you can learn is how to *survey* reading material before you read it carefully. When you survey, you look quickly through the reading material to gain a sense of the gist and organization of the chapter, article, book, etc.

A *chapter survey* gives you a "skeleton" of what the chapter covers. To survey a chapter, read and think about:

> the title
> the introduction
> the headings and sub-headings
> the summary

A *book survey* tells you what the book is about and what parts of the book you can use to help you learn. To survey a book, read and, when appropriate, think about:

> the title
> the author(s)
> the date of publication
> the introduction and/or preface
> the table of contents

Also, find out if the book includes an index, a glossary, or an appendix. Do the chapters in the book have introductions and/or summaries?

You can use your survey of a reading assignment to give purpose(s) to your reading.

LEARNING STUDY SKILLS ON YOUR OWN: III

Surveying and Research Papers

You'll find *surveying* a very useful skill when you work on research papers. One of the major problems you need to solve in writing a research paper is choosing which sources to use. The card catalogue, *Reader's Guide to Periodicals,* and any bibliography handed out by your instructor can provide you with many potential sources. However, you need to evaluate them to see how helpful they are for your particular topic.

When you are examining possible sources for a paper, you can survey them to gain a sense of what they are about. This survey can help you discover which sources are directly related to your topic and of most use. It can also save you a lot of time.

The next time you begin a research paper, remind yourself to use surveying as a way to select the most helpful sources.

UNIT IV: THINKING ABOUT NEW WORDS

UNFAMILIAR WORDS: WHAT DO YOU DO?

When you are reading and come to an unfamiliar word, what do you do? Do you ignore it and read on? Or do you stop and try to get its meaning?

Read the passage below about the evacuation of Dunkirk during World War II. Then, answer the question beneath the passage.

> As the *evacuation* went on, the steady decrease in the number of troops, both British and French, was accompanied by a corresponding *contraction* of the defense. On the beaches among the sand dunes, for three, four, or five days *scores* of thousands of men dwelt under *unrelenting* air attack. And each of them wondered if he would be among those *exscinded* from escape.

If any of the underlined words in the passage above were unfamiliar to you, how could you learn their meanings? On the lines below, briefly *describe* how you could figure out the meanings of these unfamiliar words.

_____

_____

_____

_____

_____

LEARNING ABOUT UNFAMILIAR WORDS

When you know several ways to figure out the meaning of unfamiliar words, you can learn from textbooks, articles, and other sources more effectively. Three useful methods for learning about unfamiliar words in your reading are:

1. Use of *context:* figuring out the meaning of unfamiliar words by using surrounding words in the passage
2. Use of *structure:* figuring out the meaning of unfamiliar words by using word parts, such as prefixes, roots, and suffixes
3. Use of a *dictionary*

USING CONTEXT

The *context* of an unfamiliar word includes the words and sentences which surround it in a passage.

Context clues are specific words, phrases, and structures which can help you use the context more effectively. *Context clues* can also involve ways of thinking about a passage so that you can make better sense of its unfamiliar vocabulary.

In the next few practices, you'll learn about a variety of helpful context clues.

DIRECT CONTEXT

Figuring out word meanings through *direct context* is easier than looking words up in the dictionary. And the meanings are often clearer. A direct context clue conveys a meaning which makes immediate sense to you. It's a "dead give-away."

Practice 1: Below are four kinds of *direct context clues* and examples of each. Study clue #1 and its example. Then, read sentence A below the example. Circle the context clue in the sentence, and underline the words which tell you the meaning of the unfamiliar word in capitals.

Use the same procedure for clues #2–4.

The clues begin below.

CLUE #1: The author uses the word "is" or the words "that is," "means," etc. as he or she begins to define a term.

Example: By ROLE we mean the script for behavior approved by society and appropriate to a given status.

        clue: we mean

        role = the script for behavior approved by society and appropriate to a given status

A. Copper and gold are MALLEABLE; that is, they can be beaten flat without breaking.

CLUE #2: The author uses an appositive, often with the word "or". (An appositive is a term which explains or identifies another term in the sentence. Example: Peter Harris, the bank manager, ran off with $1,000,000. "The bank manager" is an appositive, another way of explaining who Peter Harris is.)

Example: She had never before heard of an OCTARCHY, or a government by eight rulers.

        clue: comma indicating appositive, and word "or"

        octarchy = government by eight rulers

B. All primitive societies seem to have some PUBERTY RITE, a ceremony of transition from the child role to the adult role.

CLUE #3: The author places the meaning in parentheses beside the word.

Example: The child learns these expectations in many ways, directly by SANCTIONS (reward or punishment) and examples and indirectly by forces in the environment.

        clue: parentheses

        sanctions = reward or punishment

C. Socialization begins only after the TUTELARY (guardian) spirit or spirits have "chosen" him.

CLUE #4:   The author uses dashes to set off the meaning of a term.

Example: An ALLUSION — a reference to something in history or previous literature — is, like a richly connotative word or symbol, a means of suggesting far more than it says.

> clue: dashes
>
> allusion = a reference to something in history or previous literature

D: He performed EXPERIMENTS — that is, he asked nature direct questions in the form of planned manipulations — rather than observing and then speculating.

Practice 2:   Use direct context to figure out the meaning of each capitalized term in the sentences below. Underline the word(s) in each sentence which conveys the meaning to you.

1. SOCIALIZATION is the process by which children learn the rules and expectations of their culture.

2. Fundamental alteration in the nature and structure of a substance is a CHEMICAL CHANGE.

3. Iron in pure form (WROUGHT IRON) is not very hard.

4. Joined by adventurers from all nations, these Dutch sailors fared forth in ships specially designed with shallow drafts — the famous "FLYBOATS" — to navigate the shallow coasts and estuaries of the Netherlands.

INDIRECT CONTEXT

Figuring out the meaning of an unfamiliar word through *indirect context* is like detective work. Sometimes you find useful clues in the same sentence as the unknown word. But often you also need to examine other, surrounding sentences.

Practice 3:   Below are five kinds of *indirect context clues* and examples of each. Study clue #1 and its example. Then, read passage A below the example. Use the passage and the context clue to help you figure out the meaning of the unfamiliar word.

On the appropriate lines below the passage, explain how you figured out the meaning of the unfamiliar word and what the meaning is.

Follow the same procedure for clues #2–5.

The clues begin below.

CLUE #1:   Experience clue   By relating your own experience to the context, you figure out the meaning of the unfamiliar word.

Example: When the Germans approached the block, Fella quickly hid in the closet by her bed and watched through the CHINK in the closet door.

> explanation: We know she is hiding in a closet. We can guess that a chink is a small opening.
>
> chink = small opening

A. The fight wasn't on the air, so there was no need for the PUNCTUALITY required by the radio business. (Later I read in the newspaper that the bout had been delayed in deference to the hundreds of people who were still in line to buy tickets and who wanted to be sure of seeing the whole fight.)

explanation: _____

_____

_____

punctuality = _____

_____

CLUE #2:   Mood and tone clue   The mood or feeling which a passage creates helps you gain an understanding of an unknown word.

Example: From my window, through two panes of clumsy, billowing glass, a corner of this university, this city, this BROODING country. The Kremlin in the distance, the jewel of possessed autocrats, shrouded in an icy fog. Around it, the central quarters of the city, leaden and SULLEN to match the natural setting. Frozen steam rising from the ice packs in the Moscow River, drifting, darkening, and settling in the expanse of a deserted Lenin Stadium.

explanation: Terms like "shrouded in icy fog," "leaden," "frozen," "darkening," and "deserted" give the idea of sadness for the words "brooding" and "sullen."

brooding = sulking, gloomy

sullen = dismal, gloomy

B. She was not only singing, she was weeping, too. Whenever there was a pause in the song, she filled it with gasping, broken sobs and then took up the lyric again in a QUAVERING soprano.

explanation: _____

_____

_____

quavering = _____

_____

CLUE #3:   Example clue   Sometimes the author lists examples to illustrate or clarify her or his meaning. When you understand the examples, you can infer the meaning of an unfamiliar word from them.

Example: But he's also FRUGAL: goes to the movies alone; presses the pants of his single, coarse black suit; cuts an old piece of the cheapest grade of sausage into the potatoes for his dinner.

explanation: All the examples indicate that the man is trying to save money.

frugal = thrifty

C. The sound in the car shop was EXCRUCIATING. Lathes, metal drill presses, table and band saws for wood, and hand drills at several work benches were running simultaneously.

explanation: _____

_____

_____

excruciating = _____

_____

CLUE #4: Words in a series or parallel words clue

Sometimes the unknown word fits into a pattern with other words, and you can figure out its meaning from examining that pattern.

Example: It was like a train station parting. All of the political anger, the racial differences, and the age DISPARITIES vanished in the exchange of autographs, in people connecting, even when they know that so much of what society is and stands for keeps them distanced, and keeps their unborn children distanced.

explanation: Each phrase in the series refers to kinds of differences. They are political anger (a difference of opinion), racial differences, and age disparities.

disparities = differences

D. He seems to make a living. He is no idler, LOLLYGAGGER, or bum.

explanation: _____

_____

_____

lollygagger = _____

_____

CLUE #5: Opposite word clue

Often the unknown word is set in direct contrast to one you know well. Look for words like "but" which indicate contradiction.

Example: If I had been drowsy a few minutes before, this feeling had totally vanished, giving way to a state of extreme LUCIDITY.

explanation: He had been drowsy, but that feeling had vanished. Now he must be wide awake.

lucidity = clearness

E. But that was the last touch of AMIABILITY that I was destined to see in Bryan. The next day the battle joined and his face became hard. By the end of the week he was simply a walking fever. Hour by hour he grew more bitter.

explanation: _____

_____

_____

amiability = _____

_____

Practice 4: Use indirect context clues to help you figure out the meanings of the capitalized words in the sentences below. Write each meaning on the line provided.

1. And perhaps it is because she had said it to him so simply and INGENUOUSLY that he felt himself so obligated.

   ingenuously = _____

   _____

2. He had been sociable. Now he was MISANTHROPIC.

   misanthropic = _____

   _____

3. This freedom in Fella's manner, her ability to rouse in him a manly sense of honor — and in a place like this, when all around him soldiers were WALLOWING like swine in mud — all this opened up in him LATENT, forgotten feelings which elevated him above his surroundings.

   wallowing = _____

   _____

   latent = _____

   _____

4. This dark region in him, fate-ruled, where nothing was true but horror, was expressed INARTICU-LATELY, in brief, bitter exclamations, or phrases of rage, incredulity, betrayal.

   inarticulately = _____

   _____

5. Then they were INCENSED; it was unprecedented, outrageous, to challenge the leadership at an open meeting.

   incensed = _____

   _____

STRUCTURE

Some words can be broken down into parts called prefixes, roots, and suffixes.

> *Roots:* give the basic meaning of the word; may comprise the entire word or may be found at the beginning, middle, or end of a word.

> *Prefixes:* give meaning at the beginning of a word.

> *Suffixes:* give meaning at the end of a word.

Practice 5: Read the description of the root, *gen,* and the examples. Then, complete each of the sentences below with one of the examples.

Gen is a root which means birth, race, or kind. It is used to form many words.

> *Genetic* means having to do with the origin, birth, or development of something.

> *Generation* refers to individuals born and living at a particular time.

> *Genocide* means killing a race.

1. Hitler committed _____ when he ordered the killing of millions of Jews.

2. A _____ change is one which occurs as a result of heredity.

3. When parents teach a tradition to their children, they are passing it down from one _____ to the next.

Practice 6: Read the description of the root, *cide,* and answer the questions below.

Cide is a root which means kill. Below you'll find three other roots which can be combined with *cide* to form words:

> mater = mother
>
> frater = brother
>
> homo = man

1. Which two roots above mean killing another human being?

    _____ + _____

2. Which two roots mean killing one's mother?

    _____ + _____

3. Which two roots mean killing one's brother?

    _____ + _____

4. Note that the spelling of some word parts changes as the part is used in different words. Example: frater; fraternal; fratricide. How would you spell the words which you made to answer questions #1 and #2 above?

    1. _____   2. _____

Practice 7: Read the definitions and examples of the prefixes listed below. Then, complete each of the sentences below with one of the examples.

Pre- is a prefix meaning before.

     Precondition means a condition which exists before something else can exist.

Re- is a prefix which means back or again.

     Regeneration literally means to be born again.

1.   In biology _____ is regrowth of parts which have been destroyed.

2.   An organized society is a _____ for the development of science.

Practice 8: Read the definitions of the three suffixes below. Then, add one of the suffixes to the under-lined word part in sentences #1–3. You may need to add extra letters to complete the words.

-ic: an adjective suffix meaning *like,* or *being related.*

-ly: an adverb suffix meaning *in the manner of.*

-tion: a noun suffix meaning *the quality of* or *action of.*

1.   He is suffering from a ____gene____ disease.

2.   Animals adapt ____genetic____ to their environments.

3.   The young ____gene____ wants to live in a peaceful world.

USING STRUCTURE

Defining words by structure may give you a definition which sounds artificial. Still this definition based on structure often helps you to gain a clear idea of a word's meaning.

CONTEXT PLUS STRUCTURE

Like detectives, effective readers often use more than one type of clue to solve a word meaning problem. When you apply both structure and context clues together, you'll be able to figure out the meanings of many unfamiliar words.

Practice 9: Read the sentences below. Note that certain word parts have been defined. Use both structure and context clues to help you write definitions of the underlined terms.

1.   Some nineteenth century biologists held that a cell surface was merely an *interface* like the one that exists between a water droplet and the surrounding air.

     inter = between

     Define *interface:* _____

_____

2. As a consequence, a natural population in a natural setting eventually arrives at some kind of *equilibrium* in which *displacement* through death is relatively balanced by replacement through birth.

equi = equal	libra = balance	dis- = apart, reversal, remove
place = place	–ment = act of	

Define *equilibrium:*_____

_____

Define *displacement:* _____

_____

3. Each living system is tuned at once to maintaining constancy while testing *innovations.*

in- = in	nova = new	-tion = quality of, action of

Define *innovations:* _____ _____

_____

USING A DICTIONARY

When you can't define a word by using context and/or structure, turn to a college dictionary. A paperback dictionary is handy to carry around, but you'll need a college dictionary to help you with the vocabulary which you'll encounter in college courses.

Use the dictionary to find the meanings of words and word parts. You can also use the dictionary to help you pronounce, spell, and identify the part of speech of a word.

WORDS AS CONCEPTS

A college instructor rarely asks for a simple definition of a word. Rather, most instructors expect students to demonstrate understanding of a word or term as a *concept.*

When you understand a word as a concept, you can define it and explain it. You can give examples of the word's meaning and also apply it to a real or theoretical situation.

Only when you understand a new word as a concept can you say that you've included that word in your vocabulary.

UNIT IV SUMMARY: THINKING ABOUT NEW WORDS

When you come across unfamiliar words in your reading, you need to find out what they mean if you wish to understand what you've read.

One way to define an unfamiliar word is by using its context. *Direct context* means that the unfamiliar word is clearly defined within the text. Several direct context clues are:

- a. words like "is", "that is," "means," etc.
- b. appositives
- c. parentheses
- d. dashes

Indirect context means that the unfamiliar word is only indirectly defined in the text. To use indirect context, you must play an "educated guessing" game using clues such as:

- a. Your own experience
- b. The mood and tone of the passage
- c. Examples of the unknown term
- d. Words in a series which are roughly synonymous with the unknown term
- e. Words with meanings opposite to the unknown term

Another way to learn about the meaning of an unknown word is through its *structure.* With some words you can examine their prefixes, roots, and/or suffixes to help you figure out their meanings.

Sometimes using *context plus structure* can help you to define an unfamiliar word.

If neither context nor structure offer enough information about the meaning of an unfamiliar word, you need to use your dictionary.

When you have learned how to use context, structure, and the dictionary, you'll have gained a repertoire of skills for building your vocabulary.

LEARNING STUDY SKILLS ON YOUR OWN: IV

More About Learning Style

Learning style is a concept with which educators have worked for only about fifteen years. That makes it a fairly new idea, although it begins to explain differences in learning which people have known about for a long time.

There are many researchers investigating learning style now, and so there are a variety of models or systems which try to make sense of learning style differences. One particularly useful one, the work of Rita and Kenneth Dunn, is shown below.

DIAGNOSING LEARNING STYLES

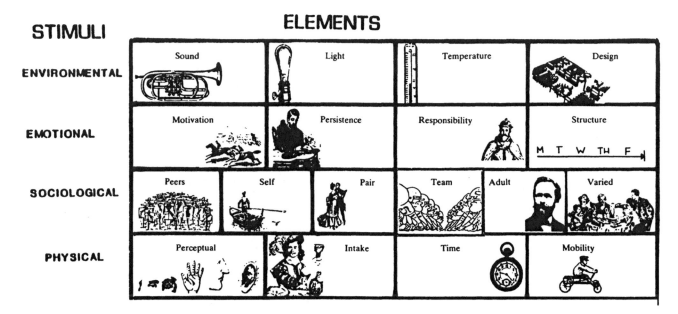

Most of the categories above are clear, but a few do need explanation. DESIGN refers to the kind of furniture you use and how you place yourself when you're learning. For example, when you're reading, do you sit up, recline, or lie down? STRUCTURE means the extent to which you can organize and pace your learning on your own and the number of guidelines and controls you need from others, e.g., teachers. For example, can you work on a project gradually for four or five weeks and complete it on time? Or does it help you to have some part of that project due every week? INTAKE refers to whatever you take into your body while you learn, for example, food or drink. MOBILITY means how much you need to move around while you are learning.

You can use a model like this one to help you become more aware of what aids and hinders your learning. Think about each of the categories and what you know about your needs and preferences as a learner. Ask yourself questions like these:

> What kinds of learning do I do well with others, and what kinds do I do better alone?

> What really motivates me to learn, and how much can I choose to be motivated?

> When I'm reading, in what position do I learn best?

The Dunn's model of learning style is excerpted from their book, *Teaching Students Through Their Individual Learning Styles: A Practical Approach,* by Rita and Kenneth Dunn (Reston, Virginia: Reston Publishing Co., 1978). If you want to learn more about learning style, you may wish to take a look at this source. Also, check the *Reader's Guide To Periodicals* and your library's card catalogue for other resources.

UNIT V: ASKING USEFUL QUESTIONS

INTRODUCTION

Imagine that you are learning about something new to you. Do you ever ask yourself questions as you go along and then answer them? Many people do. Others use a question-and-answer process without really being aware of it.

Asking and answering questions about what you are studying is a powerful tool for learning. It can help you in the following ways:

1. Asking and answering questions is an *active* process. It involves you in what you are doing.

2. Asking questions helps you to *focus* on what's really important in what you are studying.

3. Asking and answering questions helps you to *concentrate* on your learning and to *remember* more effectively.

If you already ask questions while you study, this unit can help you to make your questions more useful. If you don't ask questions, the activities of this unit can help you learn about what kinds of questions to ask.

LITERAL QUESTIONS AND EXPLORATORY QUESTIONS

Most questions that you'll ask fit into two categories: *literal questions* and *exploratory questions.*

Literal questions refer to ideas, concepts, and data which are directly stated in a book, article, or lecture.

Exploratory questions are ones which go beyond what is stated and deal with implications, meanings, and your own interests and curiosity.

For example, in regard to the article "The Historical Sources" in Unit II, a literal question might ask: "What materials and methods of study can tell us about the lives of the poor throughout the history of European civilization?" An exploratory question might ask: "To what extent are these methods useful for studying the history of other cultures?"

Different students will tend to create similar literal questions about a reading or lecture, because literal questions are tied directly to the ideas, concepts, and data in a presentation. Exploratory questions tend to vary more according to your own interests and concerns.

Practice 1: Read paragraph #1 below. Then, circle the letter of the question which you find to be the most useful *literal question* about this paragraph. Follow the same procedure for paragraphs #2 and #3.

1. In time gunpowder helped to destroy the medieval order of society by giving armies a means to level castle walls, and the man on foot a chance to shoot down a horseman in armor. It was the earliest symbol of the technological proficiency that was to lead European armies to the conquest of other continents during the five centuries from 1400 to 1900, a conquest that is being reversed only in our own lifetimes.

   a. How did gunpowder destroy the medieval order of society, what was it a symbol of, and when?

   b. What was the earliest symbol of technology?

   c. What historical role did gunpowder play from the Middle Ages on?

2. An important task confronting the adolescent is the development of a sense of his own *identity* — a conception of who he is and where he is going. To find out who he is, he must formulate standards of conduct for himself and for evaluating the behavior of others. He must know what he values as important and worth doing. And he needs a sense of his own worth and competence.

   a. What does the concept of "identity" mean in terms of adolescent behavior?

   b. How does the adolescent find out who he is?

   c. How important are values to identity?

3. Naturally occurring compounds of ever-increasing complexity were synthesized after Perkin. The synthetic substance, to be sure, could not compete with the natural product, in any economic sense, except in relatively rare cases, such as that of indigo. However, the synthesis usually served to establish the molecular structure, something that is always of vast theoretical (and sometimes practical) interest.

   a. What synthetic substance could compete economically with the natural one?

   b. Why was the synthesis of products important to science?

   c. Why couldn't synthetic products compete economically with natural ones?

ASKING LITERAL QUESTIONS

An effective literal question includes these characteristics:

1. It asks about main ideas and important details which are directly expressed in a passage or section.

2. It is comprehensive; that is, the question elicits an answer which includes all of the important ideas stated in the passage or section.

3. It is clearly expressed.

Useful questions often begin with words like these: *who, what, how, where, why,* and *when.* Yet effective "questions" need not be questions at all; they can be statements which require a response. Such "questions" often begin with these words: *state, define, trace the development of, list, analyze, compare* and *contrast,* etc.

ASKING QUESTIONS AND READING A TEXTBOOK

You can use literal questions when you read any printed materials with headings, for example, a chapter from a textbook or an article from a journal or magazine.

When you begin to read a chapter or article, the title gives you an initial idea of its subject. After that you need to discover *who* or *what* the first section is about. Then, you need to find what important *information* or *explanation* this section gives about the *who* or *what.* As you read through the chapter or article, you repeat this procedure with each new section.

Many textbooks and articles emphasize the subject, the *who* or *what,* in boldface headings. Or, they begin each section of text with a question which is answered in that section. When you learn to turn headings into useful questions, or use the questions given, and then answer them, you will make your reading more active and focused.

Practice 2: Below you'll find a list of section headings from textbooks. Turn each heading into a question which would help to direct your reading of that section of the chapter.

1. The Photoelectric Effect

_____

2. Bullionism

_____

3. What Determines A Person's Problem Solving Ability?

_____

4. Pasteur's Discoveries With Tartaric Acid Salts

_____

5. How Covalent Bonds Hold A Water Molecule Together

_____

WRITING YOUR OWN LITERAL QUESTIONS

When a chapter or article has no headings, you can generate your own questions.

1. When the topic sentence in an introductory paragraph is easy to find, you can often turn that into a useful question for the whole section or passage. Or, read the introductory paragraph(s), and formulate a question based on the main idea conveyed.

2. When the introductory paragraph(s) does not offer you a useful question, read through the passage or section to find its main ideas and supporting details. Then, ask a question, the answer to which will be these main ideas.

Asking helpful questions can be difficult at first. Often it helps to work with a partner so you can share your ideas. With practice, you can learn to ask very helpful questions about your reading.

Practice 3: Write one literal question which can help you focus your reading of each paragraph below. Once you've asked a question and read the paragraph, then tell yourself the answer to that question.

QUESTION for Passage A

_____

_____

_____

A. Preparations for Portuguese expansion began in 1419, the year Prince Henry established a center for the study of navigation and seamanship at the village of Sagres on the southwestern tip of Portugal, overlooking the Atlantic. There he brought together academicians and men of practical experience: astronomers and geographers, cartographers, instrument makers and ship builders, travelers and sailors, men of various nations, particularly Italians, Jews, and Arabs. With their knowledge and the crown's money, a systematic program of discovery and exploration was launched. Henry pursued the task with single minded devotion throughout his life. His inspirational leadership, his genius for organization and planning, his unflagging confidence, and his skill in justifying his expenditures to the king were indispensable ingredients of his ultimate success. Indeed, there would have been no Portuguese expansion, and thus no Portuguese empire, without Prince Henry. And he never took a voyage himself.

_____

_____

_____

B.   Some bacteria reproduce by *budding,* a process in which a small protuberance appears on the parent cell, enlarges, breaks off, grows a whiplike "tail," and swims away. During the budding cycle, the hereditary material doubles and then divides, and one part then migrates into the newly forming bud.

ASKING EXPLORATORY QUESTIONS

While literal questions address the main ideas and details conveyed in a passage or chapter, exploratory questions relate to meanings, implications, and your own curiosity and interests. These questions go beyond what is stated in your reading and involve analysis, critical and creative thinking, and discovery. Often exploratory questions arise from your own concerns and your own thoughts.

Exploratory questions often sound like these:

What does _____ mean?

How does _____ connect with _____?

What happens to _____ if I change _____ like this?

This author's argument is not convincing to me. What causes me not to believe him/her?

What else do I know about _____?

What else do I want to learn about _____?

When you read and listen, become aware of the exploratory questions that you ask yourself. Or, if you don't already ask questions, try to do so. Jot your questions down, and then follow through by answering them as well as you can. Working with exploratory questions is one of the most engaging and satisfying ways to learn, because you are learning what you have chosen to learn.

ASKING QUESTIONS AND TAKING NOTES

When you ask questions as you read or listen, you can use your questions to organize your notes. Write the question on the left side of the page, the answer(s) on the right side. Below you'll find two different ways to organize notes using questions.

Question I	I. Main idea
	A. Detail
	B. Detail
	1. Sub-detail
	2. Sub-detail
	C. Detail
Question II	II. Main idea
	A. Detail
	B. Detail
Question III	III. Main idea
	A. Detail
	1. Sub-detail
	2. Sub-detail
	B. Detail

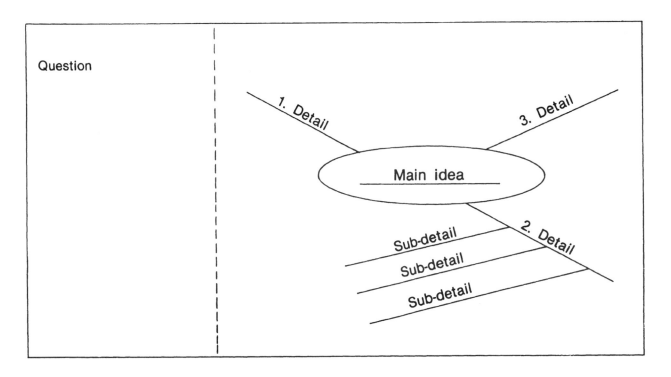

Practice 4: Read the article below. As you read, ask yourself useful questions. Answer your questions by taking notes on page 43. Use one of the methods illustrated on page 41, or another method which uses the question-and-answer format. Include both literal and exploratory questions.

CAUSES OF THE REVOLUTION

By Shirley Barrett

Was the American Revolution really necessary? Was a three-pence tax on a pound of tea so terrible that only warfare could right the wrong?

The real causes of the war are difficult to unravel — they twist and tangle like knots in a fishnet — but a quick glance backward to colonial times might put those early events into a helpful perspective.

They were people of the sea, our colonial countrymen. The lifeblood of the residents of the 13 colonies that stretched like a chain along the Atlantic shore depended on the tall ships that sailed the ocean trade lanes of the world.

The taxes the colonists paid as British subjects assured their ships protection on the high seas and in every port. Protection from greedy neighbors was also theirs by right of citizenship: from the French in the Canadian northlands, Spaniards to the south, and hostile Indians everywhere. In this they were no different from other citizens of the British Empire.

But unlike their English cousins, the Americans developed a unique tool that sent them on a different, more self-reliant path: the town meeting. They discovered, through experience and practice, that together they could tackle more difficult decisions than whose sheep should graze on the village green on Mondays. They became accustomed to having a voice in government, and when that voice was ignored the first steps on the road to independence were taken.

Many early regulations meant hardships for the colonists. The White Pine Act, for example, reserved those valuable timber trees as the King's personal property. To cut down a white pine, no matter how great the need, was punishable by law.

Nevertheless, the colonists were reasonable people. They knew that rules and regulations, laws and taxes were necessary for the smooth running of society. They agreed with Benjamin Franklin's comment in 1760: "While the government is mild and just, while important civil and religious rights are secure, such subjects will be dutiful and obedient. The waves do not rise but when the winds blow."

Storm signals, however, were already flying. Massachusetts citizens rose in an uproar when customs officials, cracking down on smuggling, were authorized to enter and search homes. Their rights as British citizens were being trampled on, they felt, but their protests were answered only with more severe legislation.

Fears of losing civil rights grew stronger as gales of British power swept through the colonies. The Townshend Act, the Stamp Act, the Tea Tax — one hated, "unjust" law followed another until waves of grievances crashed against England's shores.

Yet protests are not bullets, and dissent is not a civil war. Despite their fears, the colonists were not united in displeasure with England. Indifference, self-interest, and regional pride kept them apart. The burning, in 1772, of the British navy ship *Gaspee,* chasing smugglers in Rhode Island waters, changed all that. When the arsonists were caught, promised the furious king, they would be charged with high treason and transported to England. The threat of trial on unfriendly territory frightened Virginians and New Englanders alike and led to a united front against the mother country.

At heart it was not King George III the colonists resented, but Parliament. Their hatred deepened when Parliament passed the Quebec Act of 1774, extending the southern boundary of the Canadian province to the Ohio River, thus keeping American settlers out of rich, fertile lands. Our countrymen believed this was a deliberate move to keep them poor, near the sea, and dependent on Britain.

Even though the times were, as a Philadelphia paper complained, "Dreadful, Dismal, Doleful, Dolorous, and Dollar-less," respected leaders in every colony warned against overreaction to the mounting provocations. The Boston Tea Party was not so much an act of rebellion against paying a tea tax as a desperate ploy to get Britain's attention, to awaken her to the storm clouds gathering. Church bells tolled in mourning when General Gage and his redcoated regiments closed the port of Boston and plunged Massachusetts into economic disaster; but even then Benjamin Franklin and his friends remained convinced that a shooting war was unthinkable.

The idea of war with Britain was terrifying. Centuries of tradition, affection, and loyalty to the monarchy could not be renounced easily, and many could not accomplish it at all. Divided loyalties aside, practical questions remained. How could a small force of untrained men hope to vanquish a huge army of professional soldiers? And if by some miracle America became free, who or what would reign in the King's place? Fear of anarchy was very real in 1775. America's moment of decision was at hand.

Patrick Henry saw it coming in March 1775. "There is no longer any room for hope," he said. "We have done everything that could be done to avert the storm . . ." War was inevitable, he declared, "and let it come!"

A month later, news of Lexington and Concord poured like a tidal wave over the land. George Washington took command of a ragtag militia with sorrow, doubt, and regret at the turn of events. The other George felt differently: Indignant over his subjects' audacious defiance, he proclaimed them enemies of the crown and locked them out of the British Empire forever.

Was the Revolution necessary? Perhaps not, *if* . . . If the British government had recognized the changing character of Americans faced with difficult situations on a new continent. If the British had not underestimated the resolve and resources of determined men. If King and Parliament had held the reins of authority with a lighter hand. But things were as they were, and under the circumstances, revolution, as Patrick Henry said, was inevitable.

TITLE _____

AUTHOR _____ DATE _____

THINKING ABOUT YOUR QUESTIONS

As you practice asking useful questions, you'll probably raise concerns like the ones below.

1. How many questions should I ask? Do I need to ask a question for every section of the chapter?

    Not necessarily. What's important is not how many questions you ask, but that you ask useful questions which relate to the main ideas and concepts in the reading or lecture. Try to pose as many questions as you need to help you make sense of what you are reading or hearing. Then, answer them.

2. Do I have to write down my questions?

    This depends on how you learn. If it helps you to write questions, then do so, perhaps using your questions as part of your notes. Some people just tell themselves their questions. Others write questions in the margins of the book (when they own the book).

The key to asking useful questions is learning to pose questions which help you focus on what's important in your reading or listening. Asking questions and answering them is a procedure which helps you to focus more clearly and learn more effectively.

Practice 5: Your instructor will deliver a short lecture. Use a question-and-answer method to take notes for this lecture on page 45. Include both literal and exploratory questions.

UNIT V SUMMARY: ASKING USEFUL QUESTIONS

Asking and answering questions about what you are studying is a powerful tool for learning.

Asking and answering questions (1) involves you actively in what you are learning, (2) helps you to focus on what's important in what you are studying, and (3) helps you to concentrate and remember more effectively.

Literal questions refer to ideas, concepts, and data which are directly stated in a book, article, or lecture. An effective literal question is comprehensive and clearly expressed. When you read textbooks or articles, you can use titles and headings to help you construct useful literal questions about your reading. Then, read the section below the title or heading so you can answer your question.

When you read printed material without headings or when you listen to a lecture, you need to construct your own questions.

Exploratory questions relate to meanings, implications, and your own interests and curiosity. These questions go beyond what is stated and involve analysis, critical and creative thinking, and discovery.

You can use your questions to help you organize your notes. Use the left side of your paper for questions, the right side for notes which answer the questions, as shown below.

Question I		I. Main idea
		A. Detail
		B. Detail
Question II		II. Main idea
		A. Detail
		1. Sub-detail
		2. Sub-detail
		B. Detail

LEARNING STUDY SKILLS ON YOUR OWN: V

Brainstorming

When you ask exploratory questions, there is often no single right answer. There may be several answers which are right to different extents, or there may be many answers which are equally right. Yet when people investigate exploratory questions, they sometimes don't go beyond finding the first answer that comes to mind.

Brainstorming is a way to work with exploratory questions so you go beyond the first idea that comes to mind. To begin, ask yourself the question and be sure you understand it as much as possible. Then, write down all the possible responses that come to you. Use words, pictures, diagrams, or whatever is useful. Don't judge or question or evaluate the responses; just write them down. Keep writing as long as you have new ideas.

The key to brainstorming is to let your ideas emerge without judging them. Don't worry if they're right or wrong or silly or amusing or impossible or wonderful. Just write them all down.

When you have no more ideas to include, then go back over your list. Now is the time to evaluate them, to see which ideas are helpful or enlightening and which are not.

You can brainstorm effectively by yourself. You can also use brainstorming in groups. Again the key is not to judge anything that anyone says while the ideas and suggestions are emerging. Judgment gets in the way of creativity, because it makes people feel self conscious and holds them back. So let the ideas come out first. You can always evaluate them later.

UNIT VI: LEARNING FROM YOUR READING

HOW DO YOU READ?

Have you ever examined what you actually do when you read an assignment for school? How do you begin? What's the second thing you do? The third? And so on.

For a few moments imagine that you are a student in a college Economics or Psychology course. Your instructor has assigned a chapter from the textbook for the next class, and you are sitting down to do the reading. How would you go about it?

On the lines below, briefly describe how you would go about reading an assignment from a college textbook.

_____

_____

_____

_____

_____

_____

_____

_____

_____

_____

_____

_____

LEARNING FROM YOUR READING

One of the major differences between high school and college is the amount of reading you do. There's a lot more in college. Also, you're expected to keep track of what you've read for a longer time, often for an entire semester.

Do you have a way to do your reading, learn from it, and keep track of what you need to know?

If you don't, this unit will introduce you to a method of reading print material which can help you become a more effective and efficient learner. If you already have a method of your own, use this unit to help you evaluate your own way and see if you can improve it.

As taking appropriate notes is an important part of this method for reading, the first section of this unit deals with taking notes from print material. The second section will involve you in trying out the method for reading and learning.

TAKING NOTES FROM YOUR READING

How can you keep track of a whole semester of reading assignments in a college course? Only by taking notes.

What do you need to include in notes from your reading? Only as much as you need to help you recall the main ideas, concepts, and examples in that reading. When you take notes from your reading, you want to be able to return to them a month or two later and clearly understand what they say.

As you read assignments, you probably ask yourself questions and come up with responses. Include your own questions, ideas, speculations, and so on in your notes. Notes are not only a record; they also can give you a way to think about what you are reading.

"BOILING DOWN"

One key note taking skill is "boiling down" the meaning or message of a paragraph or passage to its main idea(s). Sometimes this idea can be noted in a few words. When the text is more dense, you'll want to include more in your notes. In Practice 1, you'll have an opportunity to work with the skill of "boiling down."

Practice 1: Each lettered section (A–D) below includes a short description of one style of writing in texts, a suggestion for how to "boil down" that style of writing to its main idea(s), and a practice to be completed.

Do Practice 1 one section at a time. Read each description carefully, and then follow each direction.

A. Some paragraphs or passages are filled with data or details, but the details are used only to prove the main point, give examples, and/or add description. For a paragraph or passage of this sort, try to find the main point which the detailed information is supporting. Usually you'll only want a note for the main idea, not the details.

Read the paragraph below, and write a one sentence note for it in your own words. Or, take your note by writing down several key words. Write your note on the lines below.

> The first and most striking element of that change (in economic life in England) was a sharp rise in the output of the newly industrialized industries. The import of raw cotton for spinning weighed 1 million pounds in 1701; 3 million pounds in 1750; 5 million in 1781. That was a respectable rate of increase. But then came the sudden burst in textile technology. By 1784 the figure was over 11 million pounds; by 1789 it was three times greater yet, and still it grew: to 43 million pounds in 1799; 56 million in 1800; 60 million in 1802. So was it with much else where the new technology penetrated. The output of coal increased tenfold in forty years; that of pig iron leaped from 68,000 tons in 1788 to 1,347,000 tons in 1839.

NOTE _____

_____

B. Some paragraphs or passages are so densely packed with ideas that appropriate notes for them resemble brief outlines or maps. When the material is structured clearly, you can use that structure to help you discover what is most important in that section.

Read the paragraph below, and write notes for it in the space beneath the paragraph. Use outlining, mapping, key words, or any other note taking method which works for you.

> The term *capitalism* describes this system of profit-seeking and accumulation very well. Capital is the source of profits and hence the source of further accumulation of capital. But this chicken-egg process had to have a beginning. The substantial initial accumulation, or *primitive accumulation,* of capital took place in the period under consideration. The four most important sources of the initial accumulation of capital were (1) the rapidly growing volume of trade and commerce, (2) the putting-out system of industry, (3) the enclosure movement, and (4) the great price inflation. There were several other sources of initial accumulation, some of which were somewhat less respectable and often forgotten — for example, colonial plunder, piracy, and the slave trade.

C. Sometimes paragraphs or passages offer a clear structure but then go beyond that structure. The paragraph below is an example of this. (Please note: this paragraph summarizes a great deal of material which came before it.)

Read the paragraph below, and write notes for it in the space beneath the paragraph. Use any method which works for you.

These, then, were two important features of the manorial system. First, that the arable area was divided into two parts, one belonging to the lord and cultivated for his benefit alone, while the other was divided among the many tenants; second, that the land was cultivated not in compact fields as we know them today but by the scattered strip method. There was a third marked characteristic — the fact that the tenants worked not only their own holdings but the lord's demesne as well.

D. Some paragraphs or passages are densely packed with ideas but are not so clearly organized that you can list points easily. For paragraphs or passages like this, first look for the subject or topic, or what the paragraph or passage is talking about. Next, try to figure out what is being said about the topic. Be alert for important explanations and definitions. Finally, include an example of the concept or process being described if such an example helps you to understand and/or remember it.

First, skim (read very quickly) the paragraph below, and answer questions #1 and #2. Then, read the paragraph and take notes for yourself in the space at the bottom of the page.

The instrument used to measure hotness and coldness is the thermometer, which can take many forms. But all thermometers make use of the thermometric (temperature-measuring) property of some substance; that is, a property that assumes varying values at different temperatures. In the common mercury thermometer, mercury is the thermometric substance and the volume or length of a column of constant cross-section is the thermometric property. Some thermometers make use of the varying volume or pressure of a gas, others of the electrical resistance of a metal; still others of the electrical potential developed at the junction of two dissimilar metals. We choose such devices as thermometers because they corroborate in an approximate fashion most of our sensations of hot and cold.

1. In one word, what is the topic of the paragraph? _____

2. In a phrase, what is the author telling you about the topic? _____
_____

Practice 2: Read the passage below, and take notes for it on the right side of this page. Use any method you like.

The first thing people remember about failing at math is that it felt like sudden death. Whether it happened while learning word problems in sixth grade, coping with equations in high school, or first confronting calculus and statistics in college, failure was sudden and very frightening. An idea or a new operation was not just difficult, it was impossible! And instead of asking questions or taking the lesson slowly, assuming that in a month or so they would be able to digest it, people remember the feeling, as certain as it was sudden, that they would *never* go any further in mathematics. If we assume, as we must, that the curriculum was reasonable and that the new idea was merely the next in a series of learnable concepts, that feeling of utter defeat was simply not rational; and in fact, the autobiographies of math anxious college students and adults reveal that no matter how much the teacher reassured them, they sensed that from that moment on, as far as math was concerned, they were through.

The sameness of that sudden death experience is evident in the very metaphors people use to describe it. Whether it occurred in elementary school, high school, or college, victims felt that a curtain had been drawn, one they would never see behind; or that there was an impenetrable wall ahead; or that they were at the edge of a cliff, ready to fall off. The most extreme reaction came from a math graduate student. Beginning her dissertation research, she suddenly felt that not only could she never solve her research problem (not unusual in higher mathematics), but that she had never understood advanced math at all. She, too, felt her failure as sudden death.

Paranoia comes quickly on the heels of the anxiety attack. "Everyone knows," the victim believes, "that I don't understand this. The teacher knows. Friends know. I'd better not make it worse by asking questions. Then everyone will find out how dumb I really am." This paranoid reaction is particularly disabling because fear of exposure keeps us from constructive action. We feel guilty and ashamed, not only because our minds seem to have deserted us but because we believe that our failure to comprehend this one new idea is proof that we have been "faking math" for years.

READING AND LEARNING: WHAT'S IMPORTANT

How can you learn effectively when you read? Both research in learning and wide experience have shown that every helpful method for reading includes three key parts:

1. **PURPOSE**   The more clear your sense of purpose when you read, the more you'll be able to learn what you seek to learn from a reading assignment.

2. **ACTIVITY**   The more active you are as a reader, the more you'll be involved in what you are doing and the more you will be able to remember what you've read. In this sense, activity means thinking about what you are reading. For example, asking yourself questions about the reading and answering them, or deciding what's important in the reading and taking useful notes.

3. **REPETITION**   Going over the main ideas two or three times rather than once helps you to remember them much better.

The method for reading print material described below builds in each of these three key elements.

A METHOD FOR READING AND LEARNING

This method for reading and learning contains the following five steps:

THINKING

    SURVEYING

        READING
      and
          NOTE TAKING

        REVIEWING

1. **THINKING**

Before you begin any study, the first step is to *THINK*. Ask yourself:

> *What is my purpose in doing this? Or, why am I doing this?*
>
> > For an assignment?
> > For pleasure?
> > To learn something I want to know? Something I need to know?
>
> *What do I want to get from this?*
>
> > If you need only to gain a general sense of the reading, you probably won't need lengthy notes.
> >
> > If you need to gain detailed information, you may want many notes.
>
> *What do I already know about this topic?*
>
> > If you already know a great deal, your notes will be brief.
> >
> > If you don't know much about it, you may need more extensive notes.

2. **SURVEYING**

Now *SURVEY* what you plan to read. (You may wish to look back to Unit III to go over the steps for surveying.) When you survey, you gather a good, initial sense of what the main ideas are in the reading. Also, you gain a sense of the major questions which your reading will answer.

3. READING and TAKING NOTES

Next, *READ* the material and *TAKE* appropriate *NOTES* as you go along. Take notes in a way which fits both your style and the organization of the reading.

4. REVIEWING

Finally, when you have finished reading, take a few minutes to *REVIEW* your notes. Go over the main ideas and important examples. See if you have any unanswered questions about what you have read. If you do, try to answer them. If you can't, jot them down so you can ask your instructor about them.

When you REVIEW, you go over the main ideas in the reading a third time. This repetition helps you to learn this material more effectively.

Practice 3: Use the method described above to read the article below and on page 56. Write your notes on page 57.

THE BIG PICTURE:
COMPUTERS, LINKED TO TV-LIKE SCREENS ARE DRAWING GRAPHS, BLUEPRINTS, MAPS

In this computer age, a picture is worth a thousand numbers. The numbers traditionally have filled endless columns in computer printouts. But now people are turning to computers that convert those figures into more usable charts, graphs, and even three-dimensional images.

It's called computer graphics, and it's making computer output a lot easier for people to handle. Linked to television-like screens, computers are sketching blueprints for new products, drawing maps, providing detailed peeks inside the human body and even designing new computers. Computer graphics is one of the fastest growing application areas of computer technology.

DEVELOPMENT OF COMPUTER GRAPHICS

"People simply are not equipped to interpret all the data they're getting in the form of columns of numbers these days," says Alan H. Schmidt, director of the Laboratory for Computer Graphics and Spatial Analysis at Harvard University. Graphics, a cure for this data overload, has been around for over a decade, but it only recently became simple enough for most people to use.

Meanwhile prices have been plunging. About ten years ago the graphics terminal was built by connecting a keyboard and some special circuits to one of its storage cathode ray tubes. Pictures drawn on the screens of these tubes remain there until they are erased. In other tubes, such as those used in television sets, the picture must be redrawn continually from a description stored in a computer memory. By eliminating the need for image memory, the cost of the graphics terminal was cut from $100,000 to $5,000.

Other technology improvements have enabled computer graphics to become more versatile. Designers at many companies sketch directly on the screen of a computer terminal by using a keyboard and a special pen. Multiple-color and three dimensional, almost photographic quality images are available. One company uses screens to design new products and to determine how they should be manufactured. When the process is complete, a computer connected to the screens punches a paper tape that enables milling machines and other shop equipment automatically to turn out the product.

Another new computer system allows several architects to work simultaneously on a project. Blueprints and other images are created on a computer screen. Thus, whenever architects alter one part of a proposed building — moving a door, for instance, or a heating duct — every sketch affected by that alteration is modified automatically.

MAPS AND MEDICINE BY COMPUTER

Another use of computer graphics is in cartography, and specifically in the drawing of special purpose maps. By using computers to analyze thousands of photographs taken by earth satellites, people have been able to produce instantly maps that reveal the precise location of forests, fishing areas and other natural resources. And new ways have also been developed to combine statistical and geographical information in a computer to create maps that show population growth, incidence of diseases and economic change.

In the medical area, graphics are playing an important role by allowing doctors to examine detailed images of the soft tissues and organs within the body that, unlike bones, cannot easily be inspected through ordinary x-ray techniques. In the new method, radiation pulses through the body, but instead of forming a photographic image, it is stored in the memory of a computer that blends it with electronic snapshots taken from dozens of other positions. The process known as computer tomography, is expensive.

BUSINESS BY COMPUTER

Computer graphics has also escaped its origins as a scientific and engineering tool, and is becoming part of everyday business. For about two years, the Cadillac division of General Motors has been putting geographic data and automobile registrations into a computer that produces a map showing where every Cadillac owner lives. The division is understood to use the maps in evaluating sales performance and in locating new dealerships.

Utilities are experimenting with a similar method in locating power-generating sites and transmission lines. In this case, the graphics equipment allows a utility employee to specify the origin and destination of a proposed transmission line, and then it automatically produces a map showing several possible routes, ranking each on the basis of economic and environmental factors.

Chemical Bank in New York has hooked up a computer to a giant television screen. The screen then allows the bank staff to present up-to-the-minute charts for management meetings and to answer promptly questions about what would happen if some assumptions were changed.

Simulators for training pilots of ships and aircraft also have improved because of computer graphics. The value of most simulators is limited because they allow the trainee to approach an airport or pier in only a few ways. But with computer graphics, the possibilities are infinite. One computer simulates a 240-degree view from the bridge of a large ship. From the wheelhouse one sees a very detailed picture of New York Harbor with several ships moving independently. A pilot can maneuver his ship to avoid the others, or, if he wants, he can ram his vessel into such obstacles as the Verrazano Narrows Bridge.

NOTES

THINKING ABOUT HOW YOU READ

In your college work, you are likely to be assigned many kinds of reading material other than textbooks; for example, documents and essays, biographies and case studies. Each time that you encounter a new kind of print material, think about what method(s) you can use to help you do the reading so that you learn effectively.

And remember: the method for reading presented here is a good strategy but not the only one which works. Try it for a while, and see how it helps you learn. Then, discover if there are any ways which you can change it to make it work better for you.

A FEW MORE HINTS ABOUT TAKING NOTES

1. Write down important terms and their meanings.

2. Be as brief as possible, but be clear.

3. Use your own words as much as you can; you'll remember them better.

4. Find help from another student or from the instructor when you have trouble understanding the material about which you are taking notes.

5. Try to learn a couple of different ways of taking notes, so you can use each as the situation requires. For example, outlining, mapping, and key words all work, but each method is more useful in some particular situations.

UNIT VI SUMMARY: LEARNING FROM YOUR READING

You can learn more effectively from your reading when you use a method which includes:

PURPOSE **ACTIVITY** **REPETITION**

This unit presents such a method, which has five steps:

Thinking: Before you begin any study, ask yourself what your purpose is. Why are you doing this? What do you want to get from it? What do you already know about the topic?

Surveying: Next, survey what you plan to read to gain a sense of what the main ideas and questions are in the reading.

Reading and
Taking Notes: Read the material and take useful notes as you go along.

Reviewing: When you've finished reading, take a few minutes to go over your notes and review the main ideas and examples.

An important note taking skill is "boiling down" the meaning or message of a paragraph or passage to its main idea(s). Sometimes this idea(s) can be noted in a few words. When the text is denser, you usually need to write more in your notes.

LEARNING STUDY SKILLS ON YOUR OWN: VI

What's Your Purpose For Learning?

In college you can gain control of many of the choices that were made for you in high school. While in high school you were subject to a collection of state and local laws and policies which largely determined what you were supposed to do, in college you participate by choice.

You can choose why you are there and, to a large extent, what course of study you will follow.

Which of these inner monologues sounds more familiar to you when you think of being in school?

A. "Well, let me see. What do I have to do to do well in Geology? I have to get to class most of the time and take pretty good notes, do most of the reading and all the labs, and at least do okay on the tests."

B. "What's my purpose in taking Geology in the first place? Well, I want to learn about it because it seems like a pretty interesting thing to know about and understand, how the Earth was formed and changes and all that. And I might decide to major in it, because there are lots of interesting jobs that have to do with Geology."

The more you can learn in college for your own purposes rather than just to get good grades, the better you'll feel about what you are doing. And the more successful you'll be as a student. It may seem surprising to you, but there's a lot of research which says that the people who learn best are those who know why they want to learn.

When you make choices in college about what you'll do, keep in mind what your own purposes are. Try to learn what you want and need to learn, not just what you have to learn to get by.

UNIT VII: TAKING CHARGE OF YOUR LEARNING

WHO'S IN CHARGE?

Each of the study skills with which you have worked so far has to do with how you perceive, make sense of, and record ideas, concepts, and other information. Working with information more effectively is one aspect of what you can gain by developing study skills. Yet there is another equally important aspect of study skills. This involves how you organize your inner self to go about your learning.

Who is in charge within you when you want to learn? Do you do things mostly by habit? Do you do what seems easiest at the moment? Or do you choose how and what you intend to learn?

The more you can be in charge of your learning and choose what you intend to do, the more successful you'll be as a learner. This unit will introduce you to three ways through which you can take more control of your own learning by:

a. setting goals for yourself

b. creating a helpful study environment

c. using your time wisely

GOAL SETTING

Goals are targets towards which you aim. A goal can be as simple as planning to complete a reading assignment by a certain time or as involved as wanting to prepare in college to enter a particular profession.

Setting goals can help you take charge of your own learning. When you set a goal, you must first figure out what you want and/or need to accomplish. Then, you can use your goal to help you organize and direct your energy so you will achieve what you seek.

Practice 1: Below you'll find three incomplete statements. Complete each one by writing a goal which is real for you.

1. The course I want to do best in is _____.

2. The most important goal for my social life now is _____

   _____

3. I plan to get a grade point average of _____ this semester.

SETTING REALISTIC GOALS

For goals to be helpful, they must be realistic. You need to set goals which you can actually achieve. A realistic goal is:

a. Capable of being stated | First conceive the goal so you can state it clearly. When you state a goal, you can usually see what the first few steps are towards achieving it.

b. Believable | Set goals which you believe you can reach. When you believe that you can succeed, this positive feeling can help you achieve the goal.

c. Achievable | Set goals which you can realistically expect to accomplish given your strengths and abilities.

d. Measurable | Set your goals so they can be measured in terms of time and amount. If your goal, for example, is to finish a book by Sunday and write a five page essay about it, then on Sunday you'll know whether you've achieved it or not.

60

Practice 2: Look again at the goals you wrote for Practice 1. Is each goal clearly stated? Believable? Achievable? Measurable? If any of your goals does not meet *all four* of these standards, rewrite it on the appropriate line below.

1. _____

2. _____

3. _____

Practice 3: Now write two more of your goals on the lines below. You can write goals about school, work, relationships, etc. For each goal, describe what you see as the first step towards achieving that goal.

Goal #1: _____

_____

First step: _____

_____

Goal #2: _____

_____

First step: _____

VISUALIZING YOUR GOALS

Another way that you can help direct your energy towards achieving your goals is to visualize what success would be. To visualize means to see pictures or images in your mind's eye. When you see an image of what achieving a particular goal would be, you can use this image to help you know towards what end you are working and to move towards that end.

How do you visualize? First, state a realistic goal which you want to accomplish. Sit in a quiet place with your eyes closed. Relax, take a few deep breaths, and then ask your mind's eye to show you a picture of what it would be like to achieve this goal. Look at the picture carefully, and gain a clear sense both of what you see and what you feel.

If you lose touch with your goal later on, you can always recreate this picture to help you get back on track.

Please note: not everyone visualizes in the same way. Some people see very clear, colorful images. Others see only blurry ones or none at all. When you work with inner images or pictures, use whatever images you can create. If you practice visualizing, your images will become clearer over time.

WHEN YOU DON'T SUCCEED

Most people want to achieve all of their goals, but almost no one does. So what can you do when you set a goal and don't reach it?

Don't waste time and energy on blaming yourself. Instead, use the experience to learn as much as possible. Why didn't you do what you set out to do? Was the goal unrealistic from the start? Did other events get in the way? Were you not able to direct your energy towards accomplishing the goal?

Think about why you didn't reach the goal. Also, examine how you feel about the goal. Did your emotions prevent you from reaching it? And if so, how? Then, the next time you set a goal for yourself, use what you have learned from this experience.

Remember: failing to accomplish a goal is a waste only if you don't learn anything from the experience. When you've learned something, then it's not a failure.

YOUR STUDY ENVIRONMENT

In the Introduction to this book, you examined several elements of your own learning style, for example, how you prefer to receive information and how you like to solve problems.

Another part of your learning style involves your preferred study environment: *where* and *under what conditions* you learn best. For example, in what kind of place do you learn most effectively? Using what kind of furniture? Light? Sound? Temperature? What time of day? Before or after meals? And so on.

Practice 4: On the lines below, describe your preferred study environment: where and under what conditions you learn best. Include as much detail as possible.

_____

_____

_____

_____

_____

_____

_____

_____

_____

_____

_____

_____

Practice 5: Respond to the questions below on the lines provided.

1. Is your preferred study environment different in any way for different kinds of learning? If it is, give a few examples of how it is different.

_____

_____

_____

_____

_____

_____

2. Read over the description you wrote of your preferred study environment above. Do any changes come to mind that might make your study environment more helpful? If so, describe them on the lines below.

_____

_____

_____

_____

_____

If you suggested any changes in question #2, EXPERIMENT with them. Try them out, and see if they help you in any way. Always try to stay open to learning more about what conditions around you can help you learn more effectively.

USING YOUR TIME WISELY

A third key to taking charge of your learning is using your time wisely. With the increased workload in college, learning to *manage* your time becomes even more important if you hope to do well in school, perhaps work part-time, and still be able to enjoy yourself.

Managing your time means figuring out what you want and need to do and how to do it within the time you have. A useful tool for managing time is a schedule. Some people think of a schedule as a limitation of their choice or freedom. Actually the effective use of a schedule gives you more choice because it helps you to waste less time.

Whenever you create a schedule, remember that you are doing this only for yourself. Don't let the schedule control you. Rather, use it as a tool which helps you to accomplish the goals you've set for yourself.

CREATING A SCHEDULE

Follow each of the steps below. Create an actual schedule for the week beginning next Monday. You'll find two different schedule forms on pages 65-66. Use the one which feels most comfortable to you.

1. First list activities on the schedule which you need to do (meals, classes, work hours, sports practice, etc.).

2. List your courses on the lines below. Then, estimate the amount of time you'll need outside class to study for each subject. Write your estimates in the appropriate spaces. Then, add them to find the total.

COURSES	**STUDY TIME EACH WEEK**
1. _____	_____
2. _____	_____
3. _____	_____
4. _____	_____
5. _____	_____
6. _____	_____
	_____ TOTAL

Now, mark down times on your schedule so you have enough study time to complete your work. (You may want to give specific times to specific subjects. Or, you can vary how you use the various study times depending on your assignments. Be sure that the amount of study time on your schedule equals the total you calculated above.)

3. Mark down any other activities that you want or need to include.

4. Now take a look at your schedule and evaluate it. Does it seem reasonable and practical to you? How will it feel to follow it? Read the suggestions below, and apply them to your schedule.

   a) Try to achieve a good balance of activities in each day. Include enough time for study and "play" as well as your other activities. Also, be sure to give yourself enough time for *exercise, meals,* and *sleep,* and for *"free time."*

   b) Another part of your learning style is the *time of day* when you are most awake and alert, when you have the most energy. Are you a "morning person"? "Afternoon person"? "Evening person"? Think about your energy level at different times of day; then, plan to do your most demanding school work when you have the most energy. You can learn much more efficiently when you are alert.

   c) Plan to do at least some studying every day. You'll probably need this time to keep up with your work.

   d) Include time in your schedule for long-range assignments, like papers and projects. Plan time for long-range assignments and then use that time, so you can avoid the last minute panic.

If any part of your schedule doesn't seem right to you now, change it!

	Monday	Tuesday	Wednesday	Thursday	Friday	Saturday	Sunday
8:00 AM							
9:00							
10:00							
11:00							
12:00							
1:00 PM							
2:00							
3:00							
4:00							
5:00							
6:00							
7:00							
8:00							
9:00							
10:00							
11:00							

	Monday	Tuesday	Wednesday	Thursday	Friday	Saturday	Sunday
MORNING							
AFTERNOON							
EVENING							

USING YOUR SCHEDULE

The next step is to follow your schedule during the week you have just planned. At the end of that time, *return to this page* and use the questions below to help you evaluate your schedule.

Did you follow the schedule? If you did, in what ways was it helpful? In what ways was it not helpful? How could you improve it?

If you did not follow it, why not? How could you make a more helpful schedule for yourself?

Plan another week, and see if you can learn more about making a schedule that works for you and then using it well. REMEMBER: your schedule is only good to the extent that it helps you to manage your time, to do what you want as well as what you need to do.

On pages 69-70, you will find another copy of each schedule form. Make copies of the schedule you like, and create a schedule for each week which helps you to manage your time. For example, you may want to take a few minutes each Sunday night to plan the coming week.

Instead of using the schedules here, you may wish to buy an appointment book, and write your schedule in that. You can also use it to keep track of your assignments.

"STEALING" MORE TIME FOR STUDY

If you don't have enough time to achieve your study goals, try "stealing" more time for study in one or more of these ways:

1. Use short snatches of time — five to ten minutes on the train, at work, etc. — to review and write notes; to plan an essay; to learn formulas, vocabulary, etc.

2. Don't waste time rewriting notes, unless they are very unclear.

3. On some days wake up a half hour early, and use that morning time for study.

4. Add more weekend study time. For example, if you study effectively every other Sunday afternoon and evening, you'll probably find yourself keeping up to date. After you study on Sunday, reward yourself. Give yourself time to listen to music, go out with a friend, or whatever you enjoy. Try to give yourself a reward whenever you study hard.

Practice 6: Can you think of other ways to "steal" time for studying? Write your ideas on the lines below.

_____

_____

_____

_____

_____

WHEN YOU STILL NEED MORE TIME

When you've tried "everything" and you still lack enough study time to meet your goals, take a careful look at what you're trying to accomplish. Are you trying to do too much? You may need to cut back on your work hours or on the number of courses you're taking.

Examine your goals and schedule carefully, talk things over with a friend or a counselor, and then take some appropriate action. Don't wait until the week before final exams to decide that you are trying to do too much.

	Monday	Tuesday	Wednesday	Thursday	Friday	Saturday	Sunday
8:00 AM							
9:00							
10:00							
11:00							
12:00							
1:00 PM							
2:00							
3:00							
4:00							
5:00							
6:00							
7:00							
8:00							
9:00							
10:00							
11:00							

	Monday	Tuesday	Wednesday	Thursday	Friday	Saturday	Sunday
MORNING							
AFTERNOON							
EVENING							

UNIT VII SUMMARY: TAKING CHARGE OF YOUR LEARNING

Who is in charge within you when you want to learn? Do you do things mostly by habit? Or do you choose how and what you intend to learn? The more you can be in charge of your learning and choose what you intend to do, the more successful you'll be as a learner.

You can take more effective charge of your learning by: (1) setting goals for yourself; (2) creating a helpful study environment; and (3) using your time wisely.

Goal Setting

Goals are targets toward which you aim. For goals to be helpful, they must be realistic. A realistic goal is:

    a. Capable of being stated clearly

    b. Believable

    c. Achievable

    d. Measurable

Setting goals helps you figure out what you want and need to accomplish. Working towards the achievement of your goals helps you to organize your energies and work more effectively.

Another way to work with goals is to visualize what success would be. When you see an image of what achieving a particular goal would be, you can use this image to help you know towards what end you are working and to move towards that end.

Study Environment

Another part of your learning style involves your preferred study environment: where and under what conditions you learn best. In what kind of place do you learn best? Using what kind of furniture? Light? Sound? Temperature? What time of day? How much and what kinds of noise/quiet? Before or after meals? And so on.

Examine the environment in which you study now, and try to improve it in any ways that work for you.

Using Your Time Wisely

Using your time wisely means managing your time: figuring out what you want and need to do, and how to do it within the time you have. One helpful tool for managing time is a schedule. Rather than limiting you, a good schedule gives you more choice because it helps you waste less time.

Try creating a week's schedule and using it to see how it can help you manage your time better. Whenever you create a schedule, remember that you are doing this only for yourself. Use the schedule as a tool which helps you accomplish the goals you've set for yourself.

LEARNING STUDY SKILLS ON YOUR OWN: VII

Your "Inner" Environment For Learning

In this unit you examined your study environment, the physical setting in which you learn. But you also have an "inner" environment for learning, how you feel when you are trying to learn.

How people feel is as important to learning as how they think. Many people believe that they really have no control over their feelings, but that's often not true. When you study, you can often choose to create a positive feeling about what you seek to learn. To accomplish this, take a few minutes before you start your studying to do the following:

1. First, sit comfortably. Close your eyes and take several long, slow, and deep breaths. Begin to feel very relaxed: not sleepy in any way but awake, aware, and relaxed. Or, you may want to relax by relaxing different parts of your body in sequence. For example, first become aware of your toes and feet and feel them relax. Then, become aware of your ankles and calves, and feel them relax. Keep going all the way up your body until you reach your scalp.

   Take 1-2 minutes to relax.

2. Next, recall a positive learning experience that you've had. Remember a learning experience which was pleasant, joyful, and helpful. If you can, both see a clear mental picture or image of that experience and try to feel just what it felt like. Or, if you can't see a clear mental image, remember the experience in any other way that you can and try to feel just what it felt like.

   Take 1-2 minutes to visualize and feel the positive experience.

3. Now, open your eyes, and begin your studying.

For many people, this is a helpful routine through which to prepare the "inner" environment for learning. It helps you to become aware and alert and open to what you can gain from learning.

Try it for yourself a few times, and see how it works for you.

VIII: UNDERSTANDING AND IMPROVING YOUR MEMORY

AN EXPERIMENT WITH MEMORY

Read the directions below carefully, and follow them exactly. Don't begin until you fully understand how you are to proceed.

Directions

1. Turn the book so you can read List A below. Read List A *twice.* Then, cover the list with your hand, and write down in the blanks as many words from List A as you can recall.

2. Next, turn the book so you can read List B below. Follow the same procedure for List B.

LIST A

hydrogen	hearing
ego	reinforcement
obsession	personality
cloture	sub-committee
gold	helium
neurosis	veto
boron	titanium
legislation	

How many words did you correctly recall? _____

LIST B

Elements:
iron
mercury
aluminum
arsenic
strontium

Kinds of government:
oligarchy
democracy
dictatorship
gerontocracy
monarchy

Psychological terms:
depression
therapy
psychosis
anxiety
development

How many words did you correctly recall? _____

73

HOW DOES MEMORY WORK?

Human memory works on two different levels: short term memory and long term memory.

Short term memory   This includes what you focus on in the moment, what holds your attention. Most people can only hold about 7 pieces of information in short term memory at any given moment, although some can hold up to nine.

EXPERIMENT: Read number A below twice. Then, cover it with your hand, and try to hold it in your short term memory.

A = 6593028

Most likely you can hold it as long as you choose. Now follow the same procedure with number B.

B = 573927450621

It's much more difficult, indeed probably not possible for many.

Short term memory is exactly what the name says: short term. To learn information so you can retain and recall it, you must transfer it from short term to long term memory.

Long term memory   This includes all the information that you know and can recall. In many ways it becomes a part of you. Once information becomes a part of your long term memory, you'll have access to it for a long time.

FROM SHORT TERM TO LONG TERM

How do you move information into long term memory? Two of the ways are *rote learning* and *learning through understanding.*

Rote learning means learning through repetition, mechanically, with little understanding. For example, as a child you probably memorized the alphabet and the multiplication tables by rote.

Learning through understanding involves learning and remembering by understanding the relationships among ideas and information. Rather than using *rote memory,* you use *logical memory* when you learn through understanding. For example, you use logical memory when you remember main ideas and supporting details from a lecture not because you repeat the ideas in your mind but, rather, because you understand them.

Both types of learning and memory are useful and often are used together. For example, in history you need to relate facts which you memorized by rote to your understanding of historical concepts.

THE KEYS TO REMEMBERING

You can learn to remember more effectively if you learn and use the four keys described below. Each one helps you to enter information into your long term memory.

1. CHOOSE TO REMEMBER

Choose to remember. Be interested. Pay attention. Want to learn and know. What you choose and want is an important part of learning. People learn more effectively and remember more when they are interested and want to learn.

How can you choose to remember? One way is to take a few moments to choose to learn before you read or listen to a lecture. Sit calmly, take a few deep breaths, and tell yourself with your inner voice: "I choose to remember what I learn today." Repeat this a few times, and then begin.

2. **VISUALIZE**

Visualize or picture in your mind what you wish to remember. For many people, a mental picture or visualization is clearer and easier to remember than words are. For each major concept you want to remember, create a mental picture and then look at it carefully for a few seconds. Once you've seen it clearly, you'll probably be able to recall it.

Some people don't visualize clearly. If you don't, you can learn to improve the quality of your mental pictures or images by practicing. Look at a picture, object, or photograph with your eyes; then, close your eyes and try to see it in your mind's eye. Work with this for three minutes each day. The more you practice, the clearer your mental pictures or images will become.

3. **RELATE**

Relate ideas and information you wish to remember to each other and to ideas and information you already know. When you relate information to other information, you create a chain of memories which lead to one another. The more connections within the chain, the more easily you'll be able to remember and recall the information.

You can relate information through mental pictures, words, or both. For example, if you want to remember what the mercantile system in the 18th century was, you can see an image of raw materials flowing into England from her colonies and manufactured goods returning. Then, you can relate the appropriate words to that image.

4. **REPEAT**

Repeat what you wish to learn until you *overlearn* it. Say it in your own words. Even though you've already learned something, go over it one more time. Research shows that time you spend on *overlearning* and putting ideas into your own words will pay off by making recall easier and more complete.

APPLYING THE KEYS TO REMEMBERING

In the following practices, apply the four keys to remembering. *Choose to remember. Visualize. Relate. Repeat.* Try them out and see how they work for you.

The articles with which you will work are organized in cause/effect and comparison/contrast patterns. Note how understanding the pattern of organization in an article and taking notes using that pattern helps your memory.

THE CAUSE/EFFECT PATTERN

Many articles are organized in a cause/effect pattern. When you can follow the pattern, the ideas and information are easier to remember. Causal relationships are often chain reactions: one thing leads to another. The example below will give you a clearer idea of a cause/effect pattern.

EXAMPLE

Sue and Jim wanted a good tan for the Spring Dance. The desire for a tan caused them to lie in the hot sun for four hours. This caused them to become sunburned. The sunburn, in turn, caused them to miss classes and the Spring Dance!

CAUSE	EFFECT/RESULT
Wanted tan ⟶	Lay in sun for 4 hours
4 hours in sun ⟶	Sunburn
Sunburn ⟶	Missed classes and Dance

When you read, look for words such as *cause, effect, result,* and *because* to indicate a cause/effect pattern. In the example, notice how a result or effect can be cause of something else.

75

Practice 1: Following, you'll find a short article entitled "Inflation, Education and the After-School Job." Most of this article is organized in a cause/effect pattern.

First, *choose* to learn from this article. *Interest yourself* in the article by asking yourself, "What does this say about me or people I know?"

Next, read the article. As you read, *visualize* the main ideas and *relate* them to each other and to what you already know in any ways that are helpful to you.

When you've finished the article, complete the modified outline on page 77.

For Practice 2, you'll use the four keys to remembering to help you study for a "practice quiz" about this article.

INFLATION, EDUCATION AND THE AFTER-SCHOOL JOB

By David L. Manning

In complex and far-reaching ways, inflation is devastating the lives of far too many American high school students. It saps their buying power, skews their learning habits, and subverts their values.

The most visible sign of inflation's impact on the life of the high school student is the part-time job. Working after school has become a pervasive part of youth culture. To a startling degree the part-time job has replaced the varsity team as the central focus in the lives of many high school students.

The part-time job has long been part of the growing up process; what has changed dramatically, however, is the number of hours that high school students work to cope with spiraling inflation. When the hours are totaled, part-time work often amounts to a full-time job.

Some insight into the dimensions of the problem is provided by a recent modest survey I made of the work-study habits of 148 juniors and seniors in six Connecticut high schools, essentially one classroom in each school. The schools represent a cross-section of Connecticut public high schools, including urban and suburban districts representing varying socio-economic levels. The students ranged in age from 15 to 19.

The survey results are revealing and cause for concern among parents, educators and employers. Seventy-seven percent of the students report that they work at part-time jobs. Slightly more than half are girls. Typically, the part-time job averages out to 20 hours each week. Incredibly, 11 students said that they worked 30 or more hours per week on a steady basis.

The survey indicates a strong inverse relationship between the number of hours that students work at part-time jobs and the number of hours that they spend on homework. As the number of hours on the part-time job increases, the time devoted to homework assignments decreases. Students who work after school report that they devote an average of only one hour per school night to their homework assignments. Equally alarming is the fact that three out of four of these students indicate that they have collegiate aspirations.

This growing disparity between labor for pay and study for a deferred benefit, gives rise to a condition in which students become increasingly deficient in the mastery of basic academic skills. Homework which is assigned to develop basic academic skills and concepts, if done at all, is done haphazardly or incompletely. This is hardly surprising. Only students with uncommon talents or with unusual pluck are willing and able to tackle several hours of demanding homework assignments following three or four hours of often tedious drudgery at a part-time job.

The end result is all too familiar. Increasing numbers of high school students fail to develop facility in writing, ease in linguistic form, and competence in mathematical processes. Teachers, in turn, are forced to direct their instructional efforts toward remediation in basic skill areas, and they are unable to sharpen and broaden basic skills to a point where students can begin to move beyond the basics.

As physical and mental fatigue creeps in from a steady diet of 12-hour stints of school and work, youthful effervescence gives way to languor. Yawns come earlier in the day and with greater frequency. Attention spans shorten. Youthful dispositions grow less pleasant. Tempers flare. Coping with one's teachers and peers becomes a formidable task. Frequent absence from school becomes a way to catch up on homework or to rest for the afternoon job.

Where does all the money go? Only 24% of the students I surveyed indicated that they were working to save money for a college education or for future needs; furthermore, only one student indicated that money from a part-time job was contributed to the family budget. Where is the rest of the money spent? Most of its goes to gratify the sophisticated materialistic tastes of high school students — to buy gasoline for the numerous gas guzzlers that fill the parking lots of every high school, to buy tickets for an endless assortment of rock concerts and sporting events, to buy expensive jeans and exotic footwear, and to buy a veritable smorgasbord of fast foods.

What is most troubling from this analysis is what it reveals about the needs and the values of high school students. The primary motive for part-time work appears to be indulgent self-interest. There is little evidence of a developing sense of responsibility for their own future needs, for the substantial financial sacrifices of parents, or for the instructional efforts of teachers.

Many students find themselves locked in a troubling value dilemma: While 72% of the students who work after school admit that their schoolwork suffers as a result of the part-time job, most are unwilling to deviate from the lifestyles to which they have become accustomed. Instead, the tendency is to work longer hours to maintain them. As inflation continues to ratchet up the prices of the goods and services that students work for, their purchasing power stands still, locked into minimum and subminimum wage scales.

All the while, powerful peer pressures conspire with the usual materialistic impulses to inspire them to purchase bigger and faster cars, more fashionable clothes and to finance ever more elaborate social gatherings.

In no sense are we witnessing the rebirth of the Horatio Alger ethic; if anything, we are witnessing Algerism at its worst. Money in the pocket of a young person has immediate value; the value of a high school education, by contrast, cannot be measured in such utilitarian terms. When a part-time job dominates the life of a teenager, schooling suffers. A better balance is desperately needed.

Mr. Manning teaches in a West Hartford high school.

INFLATION, EDUCATION AND THE AFTER-SCHOOL JOB

The devastating *effects* of inflation on students:

1. _____

2. _____

3. _____

Inflation *causes* students to get _____.

_____ *cause* students not to take part in _____

and to do less _____.

    Doing less _____ *causes* students to become deficient in

_____.

    This deficiency in students *causes* teachers _____.

_____ also *cause* students to experience _____

    This *causes* frequent _____.

Primary motive for part-time work: _____.

Manning's suggested cure: _____

_____

_____

Practice 2: Study your outline for four minutes to prepare for a "practice quiz." Use the four keys to remembering: choose to remember; visualize; relate; and repeat.

ANSWERS TO PRACTICE QUIZ

1. _____

2. _____

3. _____

4. _____

5. _____

Practice 3: For a few moments, reflect on how you studied for the "practice quiz." Then, briefly answer the questions below.

1. Did you choose to remember and be interested? If so, in what way did this help you learn and remember?

   _____

   _____

2. Did you visualize the main ideas? If so, in what way did this help?

   _____

   _____

3. Did you relate ideas and information to each other and to what you already knew? If so, in what way did this help?

   _____

   _____

4. Did you go over or repeat the main ideas? If so, in what way did this help?

   _____

   _____

5. Did the cause/effect pattern of the article help you to remember it? If so, in what way?

   _____

   _____

THE COMPARISON/CONTRAST PATTERN

The comparison/contrast pattern is another way of organizing an article. Often the use of this pattern is evident from the title or first paragraph.

When you recognize the comparison/contrast pattern, use this awareness to guide your reading, note taking, studying and remembering. In particular, one good way to organize notes for this pattern is to make a chart.

Practice 4: The excerpt below from a review of John Hersey's *Aspects Of The Presidency* is organized in a comparison/contrast pattern. The book presents two character sketches, one of President Harry Truman and the other of President Gerald Ford.

Read the review carefully. As you read, circle the words which indicate the comparison/contrast pattern, i.e., different, dissimilar, in contrast, etc.

Hersey had privileged access to both Truman and Ford during the times he was with them. Truman gave total freedom of observation to the author; Ford excepted his daily meetings with Henry Kissinger from Hersey's otherwise unlimited access.

It's not a surprise that the two Presidents emerge as very different kinds of people with dissimilar views of the job before them.

Hersey's affectionate and frankly admiring portrait of Truman shows a feisty, intelligent man, well versed in the lessons of history, counseled by able lieutenants, and confident of his ability to perform.

In contrast, although he found Ford to be a cheerful and pleasant person, Hersey's characterization is far from flattering. The author says of Ford, "His was a glacial caution," in a section describing Ford's passivity. Hersey continues, "The reach of Gerald Ford's historic memory was short indeed; back beyond the year 1949, when he entered Congress, it seemed to fall into a black hole." Hersey was particularly disturbed by Ford's denying him access to foreign policy discussions, characterizing the behavior as typical of Ford's passive acceptance of Kissinger's obsession with secrecy.

At first glance, Hersey's pairing of Ford and Truman seems an attempt to write the presidential "Odd Couple." In fact, there are a number of similiarities between the two men. In addition to assuming the presidency through succession rather than election, both men were perceived as rather lack-luster figures in the Roosevelt and Nixon administrations. Both came to office during tough times: Truman trying to fill the void left by the death of a beloved President and Ford trying to restore confidence to a nation badly shaken by a monumental scandal. So much for the similarities. Hersey's detailed accounts of daily life within the Oval Office point out the differences in the way the two Presidents approached problems, sought and used advice, persuaded the opposition, and made decisions. The presidential job description emerges from these pages as one which requires an incredible array of skills and talents — greeting beauty queens, placating angry farmers, and handling international crises are the stuff of which the days are made.

Hersey's book offers no solutions to the question of how to choose a good President. What it does offer through the close-ups of two very different modern Presidents, is an opportunity for us to carefully consider those characteristics which make a few of our fellow mortals "presidential."

Practice 5: Take notes for this article by completing the chart below. You may look back to the review.

POINTS OF COMPARISON/ CONTRAST	Truman	Ford
Access Hersey had		
Personality		
Background and ability		
Method of entering office		
Conditions in country when term began		

Practice 6: Study your chart above for four minutes to prepare for a "practice quiz" about the article. Use the four keys to remembering to help you. Be sure to cover the chart when you take the quiz.

ANSWERS TO PRACTICE QUIZ

1. _____

2. _____

3. _____

4. _____

5. _____

6. _____

7. _____

8. _____

MORE HINTS FOR IMPROVING MEMORY

1. Use mnemonic (memory aiding) devices such as rhymes, acronyms, and silly sentences. Examine and complete the examples below.

   a. **RHYME**

   If a "c" you do spy,

   Place the "_____" before the "_____."

   If you do not spy a "c,"

   Place the "_____" before the "_____."

   b. **ACRONYM**

   FBI   = Federal Bureau of _____

   NATO = _____ Organization

   SNAFU = _____

   c. **SILLY SENTENCE**

	King	Phillip	came	over	for	green	stamps.
(Biology) -----	kingdom	phylum	class	order	family	_____	_____

2. As you study, use your **learning style** strengths.

   If you learn well by seeing (visual learning), draw a diagram, chart, or picture, or create mapping notes. Then, see your notes, diagram, or picture in your mind's eye. Visualize it clearly, and you'll most likely remember it.

   If you learn well by listening (auditory learning), read information aloud to yourself. Or, tape record what you want to learn and listen to the tape as you play it back.

   If you learn well by doing (kinesthetic learning), try to find ways to be actively involved in your learning.

   Many people learn best when they involve several senses. Try using seeing, listening, and doing.

3. Immediately after you hear a lecture or read an article, write a short summary or brief notes of the main ideas. Then, go over them. This summarizing takes only a few minutes and will help you remember very effectively.

UNIT VIII SUMMARY: UNDERSTANDING AND IMPROVING YOUR MEMORY

Human memory works on two different levels:

Short term memory includes what you focus on in the moment, what holds your attention. Most people can only hold about 7 pieces of information in short term memory.

To retain and recall information, you must transfer it into *long term memory* which includes all the information you know and can remember.

Two ways of moving information into long term memory are *rote learning* and *learning through understanding.*

Rote learning means learning through repetition.

Learning through understanding involves learning and remembering by understanding the relationships among ideas and information.

Four keys to remembering are:

1. Choose to remember

Be interested. Pay attention. Want to learn and remember. Consciously choose to remember.

2. Visualize

Visualize or picture in your mind what you wish to remember.

3. Relate

Relate ideas and information you wish to remember to each other and to ideas and information you already know.

4. Repeat

Even though you've already learned something, go over it one more time so you can overlearn it. Be sure to say it in your own words.

Becoming aware of the pattern of organization used in an article or lecture can also help you to learn and remember. Two commonly used patterns are (1) cause/effect and (2) comparison/contrast.

Other ways to improve your memory include:

1. Using mnemonic (memory aiding) devices such as rhymes, acronyms, and silly sentences.

2. Using your learning style strengths.

3. Summarizing lectures and articles, and going over your summaries right after you write them.

LEARNING STUDY SKILLS ON YOUR OWN: VIII

A Simple Experiment With Your Memory

Have you ever investigated how your own memory works? For example, when you are seeking information — let's say a telephone number — in your memory and it's not right there, how do you search for it? And how are various pieces of information related to each other?

Here is a simple experiment you can do in a few minutes to gain a direct view of a part of your memory. It's an experiment you can do once or a hundred times.

First, sit comfortably in a chair. Close your eyes, and choose not to move, talk, or think. Be sure to stop your inner dialogue, that is, your thinking voice inside your head. In a short time (a few seconds to half a minute at most), your inner dialogue will start up again on its own. Don't stop it or force it away. Rather, just let it go along on its own, and pay attention to it. All you need to do is listen to it. Keep doing so as long as you wish.

When you choose to stop thinking and allow your inner dialogue to emerge on its own, what is revealed to you is another part of your mind and your memory. When you watch your inner dialogue in this way, what you can see is how things are connected to each other in your mind and your memory.

UNIT IX: READING FLEXIBLY

WHAT IS FLEXIBLE READING?

Many people read everything from the most entertaining mystery to the most densely written science text at exactly the same rate. They don't read flexibly at all. Despite vast differences in how difficult the reading material is and for what purpose they are reading, many people don't know how to vary their reading speed.

One of the most valuable and time-saving study skills is *flexible reading*. This skill means learning to vary your reading rate according to:

1. The *kind of material* you are reading; for example, an article from a science magazine is usually more packed with new ideas and vocabulary and, therefore, more difficult than most short stories.

2. The *purpose* for which you are reading; for example, finding one particular piece of information in a chapter can be accomplished with a much quicker reading speed than finding all the main ideas and important details in that chapter.

3. The *difficulty* of the material *for you*: for example, if you know a lot about music but don't know much about sports, you can probably read an article about music more quickly than one about sports.

Think of flexible reading as shifting into different gears depending on what you are reading and for what purpose.

Practice 1: On the lines below, list the kinds of material you read in a typical month, i.e., newspaper, telephone book, signs, history text, etc. Don't write anything inside the parentheses yet.

_____ (   )   _____ (   )
_____ (   )   _____ (   )
_____ (   )   _____ (   )
_____ (   )   _____ (   )
_____ (   )   _____ (   )

DIFFERENT RATES OF READING

Below you'll find descriptions of four different reading rates:

1. SKIMMING AND SCANNING RATE

Skimming means reading only key words, phrases, and sentences in a piece of text. It is a very fast rate through which you can gain a general sense of what the text is about, for example, in a survey. *Scanning* means quickly searching a piece of text for some particular information. It is usually an even faster rate than skimming and is used, for example, to locate information in an index.

2. RAPID READING RATE

At this rate you are deliberately reading faster than you normally read. You are consciously trying to read quickly. This rate is appropriate when you read newspapers and magazines, when you are reading only for main ideas, and when you are reading for review.

3. **AVERAGE READING RATE**

This is the rate at which you ordinarily read. Use it for material of average difficulty which you want to recall later, for example, books with literary value, articles for assignments, and selections in which you want to know details as well as main ideas. You'll often want to use this rate for text-books which are not technical.

4. **SLOW READING RATE**

This rate is slower and more deliberate than your average rate. Use it when the material is difficult and demands that you pay more attention to each word, for example, with technical articles or texts. Or, use it when you want to take detailed notes from your reading.

In actual reading, you'll find that your use of these different rates will certainly overlap. You will want to use several rates and perhaps all four while you read one chapter or article. The skilled reader changes gears often.

Practice 2: In the parentheses next to each type of reading you listed in Practice 1, write the number(s) of the reading rate(s) you would use for that type of reading. Be able to explain your choices.

> 1 = skimming and scanning rate
>
> 2 = rapid reading rate
>
> 3 = average reading rate
>
> 4 = slow reading rate

USING DIFFERENT READING RATES

In this unit, you'll practice ways of applying different reading rates to several practical reading and study situations.

One way that you already know to use different reading rates is the surveying/questioning/reading method. First you survey an article at a skimming rate, keying on important questions. Then you read at an average rate, or faster or slower as the material demands, to answer your questions.

You've already used this survey/question/read method in other units. When you try it again in Practice 3, be aware of your changing reading rate.

Practice 3: Survey the article on page 84, using your skimming rate. In the spaces below, write three questions you can use to help guide your more careful reading of the article.

QUESTIONS

1. _____

2. _____

3. _____

Now, read the article at your average rate, or slower or faster as the material requires. Answer your questions on the lines below (unless you find a question is not worth answering). If you find important information not covered by your questions, note it on the lines at the top of the next page.

ANSWERS

1. _____
   _____

2. _____
   _____

3. _____
   _____

We've Been Asked
WHAT IS THE "THIRD WORLD"?
From Top Authorities Come Answers to Questions on Topics in the News

We hear more and more about the "third world." What is it?

First off, it's not an organization in any formal sense. It doesn't even have a membership roll.

In general, what is regarded as the "third world" consists of "have not" nations, still undeveloped, whose interests don't jibe with those of developed nations in the other two "worlds" — that is, the Communist and non-Communist "worlds."

But isn't it generally credited with having a great deal of clout in global affairs? How can that be?

The "third world" has been wielding unexpected strength, partly because of sheer numbers — and partly for other reasons.

For example, look at the oil-producing countries, most of them generally listed as "third world." They are in a cartel, and their ability to impose higher oil prices on richer nations — or even reduce the flow of petroleum — has been amply demonstrated. That's real clout in a global economy so dependent on oil.

And some other "third world" nations are trying to get in on the act. They are now organizing cartels in an effort to control supply and prices of their exports — principally bauxite, copper, sugar and coffee.

Getting back to the power of numbers: The United Nations General Assembly has more and more been turned into a forum for the "third world." It now wields a majority there.

During the last session of the Assembly, a Mexican-sponsored "economic charter" — which included approval of expropriation of foreign-owned property subject only to domestic laws — was passed by 115 votes to 6, with 10 abstentions. It had solid "third world" backing.

Isn't there a tighter definition of the "third world"? After all, Saudi Arabia isn't exactly poor.

Poverty isn't the only factor. A nation is likely to consider itself on the "outside" — and thus part of the "third world" — when its people have a highly emotional conviction that, throughout history, they've been cheated by richer nations.

These people sometimes want more than just a more-equitable distribution of the world's wealth. They may want revenge for wrongs of the past.

Another way to put it: The "third world" in general is the southern poorer half of the Earth pitted against the richer northern half. You might even detect a racial connection — the darker-skinned peoples getting together to demand "economic justice" from the lighter-skinned populations.

Who are the specific targets of the "third world" revolt?

The U.S., the richest country, is always the chief target. Next in priority are Western Europe and Japan.

The Soviet Union lays claim to strong links with the "third world" because it is "socialist," anti-capitalist and anti-imperialist. Yet most of the "third world" nations consider Russia just another "have" superpower.

Mainland China insists it will never become a superpower and claims to be on the side of "oppressed" peoples." Where does it fit in?

At the U.N., "third world" nations welcome Peking's support — but are wary of China's potential power.

How did the three-world concept come about? Isn't the world supposed to be getting smaller?

Certainly, satellite communication and jet travel have in a sense been shrinking the world. But that's part of the whole problem. Now you find peoples of the "have not" nations far more aware of just how little they actually have, compared with the two other "worlds." Once they were fairly ignorant of that fact.

Today they are far more sophisticated about economics and sharing the wealth. You find the full thrust for redistribution of the world's riches centered on the poor of the "third world" rallying together against the wealthy of the "first" and "second" worlds led by the U.S. and Russia.

So to judge who's in the "third world," it's more than just a question of examining a nation's budget or trade balance.

It certainly is — and even experts have trouble fitting countries into slots.

A good way to start, though, is to separate out those countries which belong to regional alliances such as NATO and the Warsaw Pact. The remaining countries are eligible to call themselves "nonaligned."

Then you have to consider whether the people of a country are poor — and if they feel they have been abused economically or politically over long periods by "colonial" or "imperialist" powers.

Does all this talk of different "worlds" really mean anything?

Very much so. Citizens of wealthy countries, especially Americans, are being inundated with demands by people from the poorer nations for a better life.

Leaders of all walks of life in the U.S. say this is a moral challenge that cannot be ignored.

On the dollars-and-cents level, the new-found unity among the "third world" nations can mean America will have to pay a lot more for the raw materials that support its high standard of living.

Nevertheless, the world is changing fast, and so is U.S. policy. American experts hope that an acceptable adjustment — for both moral and economic reasons — can be worked out between the "have" countries and the "have nots" of the "third world."

USING YOUR RAPID READING RATE

In certain situations, you can use your rapid reading rate to help you become more efficient in your reading. When your time for reading is limited, when you only want or need to gain a general idea of what the reading is about, or when you want to get a sense of a topic before a lecture, use your rapid reading rate as follows:

1. First, survey the article, chapter, or book quickly. Use your survey to "size up" the reading. Decide which parts or sections are useful or interesting to you. (Sometimes a survey may help you decide not to read the material at all.)

2. Next, use your rapid reading rate to read the important sections of the chapter, article, or book. As you read, focus your attention on the main ideas. Don't worry about details. If you need them, you can always return to find them. And don't feel guilty about not reading every word. An efficient reader picks and chooses what she or he reads.

3. Take a minute and review the main ideas in the reading.

Practice 4: Select a chapter which you haven't read in the textbook you've brought to class. Take *3 minutes* to survey the chapter. Then, use your rapid reading rate to read as much as you can of the important sections in that chapter in *8 minutes.* You may not finish, but see how far you get.

When you stop, estimate how long it would have taken you to read all of the important sections in the chapter at your rapid reading rate. Write your estimate in the space below.

_____ minutes

Now, estimate how long it would take you to review the main ideas you've read so far in this chapter. Write your estimate in the space below.

_____ minutes

FLEXIBLE READING FOR RESEARCH

Many college courses require you to do research and write a research paper. For this task flexible reading will prove extremely valuable. You'll be shifting your reading gears again and again as you work through the various steps in writing a research paper.

For the rest of the practices in this unit, imagine that you've been assigned a research paper in your introductory Science and Society course. Although you don't know much about them, you are interested in *lasers.* So you've chosen that as your topic. The paper assignment asks you to choose a recent scientific development and investigate both what it is and one way in which people use it. You know that lasers have medical uses, so you narrow your topic to *the medical uses of lasers.* (Later you might want to narrow the topic further.)

In these practices, first you'll skim as you look for books in the *card catalogue* and for references to your subject in the *index* of a book about lasers. You'll use several rates to read and take notes from an *encyclopedia article* and from a *journal article.*

Practice 5: One use of your fastest reading rate is skimming the library card catalogue or a bibliography to find the best sources for your paper. Once you find your subject in the card catalogue or in a bibliography, you can skim all of the included entries to find the ones most likely to be helpful to you.

Skim the card catalogue entries on the next page. Place a checkmark on the line before any item which you think might be a good source for a paper about "The Medical Uses of Lasers." (For most research papers, you'll want to choose the most up-to-date sources.) When you are done, place a second check next to the item which you think will be your *best* source.

____ Allen, Benjamin. *Lasers for Communication.* Chicago: The Tower Press, 1979.

____ Arlex, Susan T. "Is Laser Surgery Safe?" *Modern Health,* XIV (June 10, 1978), pp. 85–87.

____ Bertrand, James. "Advantages of Lasers in Opthalmology." *Science for Today.* VII (July 17, 1981), pp. 67–71.

____ Collins, Richard. *Circuitry for Semiconductor Lasers.* Chicago: Scientific Press, 1982.

____ Howard, Nancy P. "How Laser Accidents Occur in the Laboratory." *American Times,* XII (1980), 17–22.

____ Jackson, Donald. *Laser Applications.* Milwaukee: University Press, 1980.

____ King, Anne P. "Lasers Used in Engineering." *Engineering Weekly,* X (March 2, 1979), pp. 12–15.

____ Richards, Mary. *Medical Uses of Lasers.* New York: Medical Publishing Company, 1982.

Practice 6: Imagine that you've located an appropriate book about lasers in the library. You'll want to turn to the book's index and skim the entries to find the information you seek.

You know that you want information about *the medical uses of lasers.* You also need some general information about *how lasers work* for the first part of your paper.

Skim the sample index entries below to find information about (1) how lasers work, and (2) the medical uses of lasers. Place a check on the line before each entry which you think will be useful to you.

INDEX FOR BOOK ON LASERS

Applications,
____   Communications, 35–40
____   Engineering, 41–50
____   Holography, 51–53
____   Medicine, 54–62

____ Applied laser principles, 3–25

____ Bloodless surgery, 55

____ Building construction, 41–45

____ Dental drilling, 61–62

____ Energy, 27–30

____ Fiber-optic scalpel, 56

____ Fire alarm system, 50

Light,
____   Fibers, 97–99
____   Waves, 15–17

____ Radio waves, 100–105

____ Surgery, 54–60

Practice 7: You might choose to read an encyclopedia article about lasers to give you some background on the topic. On pages 87–88, you'll find such an article.

Read the article *flexibly.* Place a check in the margin next to any paragraph which relates to your paper topic.

Place an X next to any paragraph which you will skip entirely.

When you have finished reading, answer the two questions on page 88.

Remember: you're interested in how lasers work and what their medical uses are.

LASER is a device that *amplifies* (strengthens) light. A laser produces a thin beam of light that can burn a hole in a diamond or carry the signals of many different television pictures at the same time. The word *laser* stands for **l**ight **a**mplification by **s**timulated **e**mission of **r**adiation.

The light from a laser differs from the light produced by other sources, such as electric bulbs, fluorescent lamps, and the sun. The light from these other sources travels in all directions. The light from a laser is highly directional. In other words, it travels in only one direction. It travels in a narrow beam, and the sides of the beam stay almost parallel. For example, a beam ½ inch (13 millimeters) wide may spread to only about 3 inches (7.6 centimeters) after traveling a distance of a mile (1.6 kilometers).

Laser light also differs from other light in terms of *frequency*, the number of vibrations of a light wave per second. The light from a laser consists of one or, at most, a few frequencies. The light from other sources consists of many frequencies. Because laser light has so few frequencies, a laser beam has a narrow frequency range on the *electromagnetic spectrum*, an arrangement of frequencies from lowest to highest.

The frequencies of a laser beam may be in only the visible region of the electromagnetic spectrum. Or they may be in only the infrared or ultraviolet regions, both of which are invisible. The frequencies of light produced by most other sources are in the visible and invisible regions of the electromagnetic spectrum at the same time. See ELECTROMAGNETIC WAVES (The Electromagnetic Spectrum).

How Lasers Are Used

The unusual characteristics of laser light make lasers a valuable tool in (1) communications, (2) industry, (3) medicine, (4) military operations, and (5) scientific research.

In Communications, a laser can transmit voice messages and television signals. It has great advantages over ordinary electronic transmitters, such as those used to produce radio and television signals. For example, a laser operates at a much higher frequency than do electronic transmitters. The high frequency of laser light enables a laser beam to carry much more information than radio waves can. Therefore, one of these beams can transmit many telephone calls and television programs at the same time.

A laser can transmit information with little interference because it produces a highly directional beam. A laser beam can be directed to fall solely on the desired laser-receiving equipment. Because the equipment receives only the laser beam directed at it, most interference is eliminated.

A laser also may serve as an efficient long-distance transmitter because of its highly directional beam. Laser beams, unlike radio waves, spread only slightly as they travel. For this reason, scientists believe a laser beam may provide an excellent communications link with spacecraft. On the earth, a laser beam may be sent from one relay station to another through a long glass fiber. The beam is reflected through the fiber and can travel great distances with little loss of energy (see FIBER OPTICS).

In Industry, the laser has a variety of uses. For example, it may be used as a source of intense heat. The sides of a laser beam are nearly parallel, and so a lens can focus the beam to a point only 1/10,000 inch (0.0025 millimeter) wide. When the beam is concentrated on such a small area, it may produce temperatures higher than 10,000°F. (5538°C). In this way, a laser beam can be used to melt extremely hard materials.

Manufacturers use short bursts of laser light to weld miniature metal parts together in electronic equipment. For example, a laser can be used to connect wires sealed inside a glass tube. In heavy industry, high-power lasers are used to weld large metal parts together. Surveyors use a laser range finder to measure distances in making maps.

In Medicine, surgeons use the heating action of a laser beam to remove diseased body tissue. The beam burns away the unhealthy tissue in a fraction of a second with little damage to the surrounding healthy area. Eye specialists use the laser to correct a condition called *retinal detachment* (see EYE [Diseases]). They aim a laser beam into the patient's eye and focus it on the retina. The heat of the beam "welds" the loose retina into place.

In Military Operations, a laser beam can be bounced off a target, such as an enemy airplane or ship, to determine its distance and speed. Laser *gyroscopes* (guidance devices) are being developed to direct bombs and artillery shells to their target. Laser range finders and gyroscopes may be used in commercial navigation as well as by military forces.

In Scientific Research, a laser has many uses. For example, it may be used to create hot gases called *plasmas*. The study of plasmas may help scientists learn to control *nuclear fusion*, the process by which lightweight atoms combine into heavier ones to produce energy. The control of this process and the use of lasers in similar research could help solve the energy needs of mankind. See NUCLEAR ENERGY (Nuclear Fusion).

How a Laser Works

Light is a form of energy that is released from individual atoms or molecules in a substance. To understand how a laser works, it is necessary to know something about the nature of atoms and how they interact with light and other forms of energy.

Every atom is a storehouse of energy. The amount of energy in an atom depends on the motion of the electrons that orbit the atom's nucleus. When an atom absorbs energy, its energy level increases, and the atom is said to be *excited*. The atoms of a substance become excited when they absorb heat, light, or other forms of energy that pass through the substance. An excited atom can return to its normal energy level by releasing its excess energy in the form of light. This release of energy is called *spontaneous emission*.

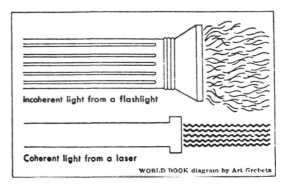

Incoherent light from a flashlight

Coherent light from a laser

WORLD BOOK diagram by Art Grebetz

Lasers Produce Coherent Light. Waves of coherent light, unlike waves of incoherent light, move "in step" with one another. As a result, they spread only slightly — even over great distances.

In spontaneous emission, excited atoms release light irregularly. As a result, the light has different frequencies and travels in different directions. Light released in this way is called *incoherent light*. Such light is produced by the sun and by ordinary electric bulbs.

Excited atoms also may release light systematically. This kind of release, called *stimulated emission,* is the main process that takes place in a laser. Stimulated emission occurs when the energy released from one atom interacts with another atom that is still excited. The interaction triggers the excited atom into releasing its own extra energy as light. Most of the light produced by stimulated emission has the same frequency as the triggering light. It also travels in the same direction, and so it combines with and amplifies the triggering light. Such light is called *coherent light.*

The basic parts of a laser include a power source and a light-amplifying substance. Stimulated emission results when energy from the power source interacts with excited atoms in the substance. The total energy produced by a laser is always less than the energy produced by the power source. But the laser produces a much more intense light.

1. The rest of the article is concerned with kinds of lasers and the history of lasers. Would you want to read these sections for your paper?

   _____

2. On the lines below, list the different rates of reading that you used for this article. For each rate, list one example of a section in the article where you used that rate.

   RATE   **SECTION**

   _____

   _____

   _____

   _____

Practice 8: Once you've read the relevant parts of the encyclopedia article, you have some basic information about lasers. At this point you may want to outline your paper, or you may choose to read further first.

Another source of information is journal articles. Read the relevant parts of the article on page 89. Be sure to *read flexibly.*

Place a check in the margin next to each paragraph which is relevant to your topic.

When you've finished reading, answer the questions on page 89.

SEEKING COHERENT ANSWERS

Laser Researchers Are Developing Coherent-light Solutions To A Host of Existing Challenges

by Janet Raloff

Every year more and more lasers are sent from the research community to be used in commerce and industry. They are already employed reading prices off products crossing supermarket checkout counters, welding detached retinas, cutting through steel and shooting three-dimensional movies. The next wave of recruits may enrich uranium, broadcast messages through the ocean to converse with submarines, or reduce the "noise" in audio and optical recordings. What follows is a glimpse of the diversity in research programs attempting to generate such recruits.

MEDICINE

Lasers entered the surgical theater during the late 1960s. Their ability to direct intense beams of energy into tissue without requiring either mechanical or electrical contact eliminated much of the trauma — such as tissue charring — associated with previous attempts to treat medical problems with heat.

So that neither a bleeding body nor a laser had to be tilted radically for a lesion or tumor to make proper contact with the scalpel-like beam, most early efforts in laser surgery focused on external tissues. But laser optics and advances in optical fibers — those flexible, hair-thin glass rods — have changed that. Carried inside endoscopes (medical instruments for viewing interior organs and canals), optical fibers now permit the intense and powerful beams of modern lasers to be curved and moved throughout the body's internal cavities without jarring a laser system's fragile and precisely aligned components. And certain sophisticated laser systems permit beam-exit ports to virtually dance over a patient's body at the surgeon's command. This resulting freedom has encouraged surgeons to explore internal use of laser cauterization and vaporization.

Richard Dwyer notes that lasers provide one of the safer ways to coagulate bleeding gastrointestinal ulcers. According to the University of California researcher at Harbor General Hospital in Torrance, "The success rate of the argon laser on selected patients is roughly 80 percent, and the success rate of the [neodymium: yttrium-aluminum-garnet laser] on unselected bleeding patients is 90 percent." What's more, endoscopic-laser surgery "can replace emergency surgery for . . . bleeding with elective surgery," Dwyer claims, adding that this procedure not only is safer for the patient, but also reduces the hospital stay required, blood transfusions necessary and days of work lost by the patient.

And for sleuthing tooth decay, lasers provide a simple and convenient tool to detect developing cavities, F. Sundstrom of the Karolinska Institute in Stockholm and H. Bjelkhagen of Sweden's Royal Institute of Technology reported at CLEO. Carious lesions in tooth enamel show up as dark spots when illuminated with blue light from an argon-ion laser. "Even initial pit and fissure lesions are clearly visible." And the procedure they developed makes it possible to spot these decay signs before they would otherwise be detectable with either visible light or ultraviolet fluorescence, they say.

DATA REPRODUCTION

Videodiscs promise to do for video what phonograph records did for sound — make prerecorded high-quality offerings available as affordable home entertainment. In commercial videodiscs today, images are recorded as a binary code spelled out in combinations of pits and spaces-without-pits. A tiny, focused laser beam burns these pits into a recording platter. To play back the images, a light passes over the disc. The presence or absence of pits triggers a photoelectric receptor to translate the encoded message into electrical signals which are eventually converted into a television picture.

1. What part(s) of the article did you skim?

_____

_____

2. What part(s) did you read in detail?

_____

_____

3. What part(s) did you omit?

_____

_____

UNIT IX SUMMARY: READING FLEXIBLY

Flexible reading means learning to vary your reading rate according to:

1. The kind of material you are reading

2. The purpose for which you are reading

3. The difficulty of the reading material for you

Think of flexible reading as shifting into different gears depending on what you are reading and for what purpose.

Four different reading rates are:

1. Skimming and scanning rate	Reading only key words, phrases, and sentences. Or, quickly searching for particular information. A very fast rate useful for surveying and finding specific information.
2. Rapid reading rate	Pushing your normal reading rate faster on purpose. Useful when you are reading only for main ideas or for review.
3. Average reading rate	The rate at which you ordinarily read material of average difficulty. Useful when you want to know details as well as main ideas.
4. Slow reading rate	Reading more slowly and deliberately than your average reading rate. Useful for difficult and/or technical reading.

For actual reading, you'll want to use several or all four rates while you read a chapter or article. The skilled reader changes gears often.

Reading flexibly can help you do research for research papers more effectively and efficiently. For example, you can skim or scan the entries in a card catalogue to find ones which are relevant for your topic. Once you locate useful books, you can skim their indexes to help you locate passages in the books which are directly related to your topic.

When you read any sources, for example, journal articles or articles in encyclopedias or elsewhere, you can use skimming, rapid reading, average reading, and slow reading as these rates are helpful to you.

LEARNING STUDY SKILLS ON YOUR OWN: IX

Speed Reading

Most people learn to read by saying single words aloud. When we take the next step and begin to read silently, we still "say" each word to ourselves in our thoughts. This is called *sub-vocalizing,* that is, "speaking" to ourselves without saying the words aloud.

Though we learn to read more complex and demanding material, most of us don't read any faster at 18 or at 48 than we did in sixth grade. Why? We continue to sub-vocalize as we read. Since we can only speak at most at about 180 words per minute, we can't read any faster than our sub-vocalizing allows.

Speed reading means learning to read without sub-vocalizing. The human mind is easily able to read without saying each word "aloud." Instead, we can learn to see words and understand them. When we learn to stop sub-vocalizing, we can increase our reading speed to 600 words per minute, 1000 words per minute, or even more. And with skilled speed reading, there is no loss of comprehension.

Of course, you can immediately see the value of speed reading in college. So how can you learn to speed read?

1. You can try to teach yourself. Work on breaking the habit of sub-vocalizing by trying to see groups of words and not saying them to yourself. If it's helpful, count as you read rather than say the words. Eventually you can let go of the counting as an aid.

   Also, teach yourself to use your hand (three fingers, two, one, or the whole hand) to underline each line of text as you read it. Move your hand lightly and quickly. Use your hand to help you move faster as you read and to keep yourself from going back over material again and again.

   Just by learning to stop sub-vocalizing and to use your hand to focus your attention and keep up your speed, you can easily *double* your effective reading rate.

2. If you need more instruction or help, find a self-taught speed reading course. One good text is *Speed Reading Made Easy* by Arlyne F. Rial (Garden City, NY: Doubleday, 1977). Or, take a speed reading course.

UNIT X: GAINING FROM DISCUSSIONS

WHY HAVE CLASS DISCUSSIONS?

Many classes in college are structured as discussions. Even some lecture courses include discussion groups once or twice a week.

Instructors use discussions to give students an opportunity to express, explore, and test their ideas, understandings, opinions, and questions. *Good* discussions provide a forum in which students and teacher can interact positively, learn from the other members of the class, and become more actively interested and involved in the subject. *Good* discussions help you to learn, and they can be engaging and enjoyable.

WHAT MAKES A GOOD DISCUSSION?

In high school, you probably participated in many discussions. Some were undoubtedly better than others. Looking back on your experience, do you know what makes a *good* discussion?

Read the two questions below. Think about them. Talk them over with your partner. Then, write your responses. (Your responses can be different from those of your partner if you don't agree.)

1. In your view, what are three or four characteristics of a *good* discussion?

_____

_____

_____

_____

_____

2. In your view, what are three or four characteristics of a *poor* discussion?

_____

_____

_____

_____

_____

THE BASICS OF DISCUSSIONS

Good discussions are interesting, engaging, and productive. To have a good discussion, you need only two ingredients:

1. Participants who discuss actively, listen well, and contribute a fair share without dominating or withdrawing

2. A topic for discussion, and ideas, information, theories, feelings, and questions relating to that topic.

In a *free discussion,* you talk about a topic in almost any way you choose. In a *guided discussion,* you respond to questions or suggestions or you solve a problem. Your course discussions will probably be more guided than free.

A good discussion doesn't require a moderator or leader, though it can be helpful to have one. In class the instructor often acts as the discussion leader.

Practice 1: Your instructor will give you directions for discussing a problem. Your task will be to find a solution to the problem.

In this practice, you'll have an opportunity to take part in a discussion in which you pay attention both to how the discussion works as a whole and to your role in it. You will also receive feedback from an observer.

For this discussion, each member of the group will have a job. The jobs are:

RECORDER: One person will take notes about what is said and agreed during the discussion.

OBSERVER: One person will observe what each participant does and says.

PARTICIPANT: All other group members will discuss the problem and try to solve it.

Each member of the group will write something either during or after the discussion. The forms to be used are:

1. **NOTES:** The recorder will take notes on a sheet of paper *during* the discussion.

2. **OBSERVER'S FORM:** The observer will mark the form on page 94 *during* the discussion.

3. **PARTICIPANT'S FORM:** Each participant will mark her or his form below *after* the discussion.

PARTICIPANT'S FORM

Directions: Use this form to evaluate the discussion. Circle the number on the scale to the right of each item. Note that the scale ranges from "yes" to "no" in four steps.

	ITEM	RATING SCALE			
		Yes			No
+	1. All members participated.	1	2	3	4
+	2. I was actively involved.	1	2	3	4
+	3. I listened carefully and actively.	1	2	3	4
+	4. I encouraged others to participate.	1	2	3	4
+	5. I added pertinent information.	1	2	3	4
+	6. I learned from the discussion.	1	2	3	4
−	7. I dominated the discussion.	1	2	3	4
−	8. I argued excessively.	1	2	3	4
−	9. I withdrew from the discussion.	1	2	3	4

Add two items of your own:

10.	_____	1	2	3	4
11.	_____	1	2	3	4

OBSERVER'S FORM

Directions: Fill in the names of your group members except for your name and the recorder's. Each time a participant speaks, place a mark in her or his column next to the role she or he played. When the discussion is done, add the marks in each box, and write the sum in the lower right corner of the box.

ROLES	NAME OF PARTICIPANT (fill in)					
1. ENCOURAGING — encouraging other members to state their ideas						
2. QUESTIONING — asking helpful questions						
3. ADDING — giving information, offering opinions and new ideas						
4. CLARIFYING — making previously stated ideas more clear						
5. SUMMARIZING — repeating ideas already stated to summarize						
6. COMPROMISING AND PEACE-MAKING — helping bring members with different viewpoints together						
7. ARGUING — disagreeing with another person's views						
8. DOMINATING — taking over the discussion						
9. WITHDRAWING — not participating						

SHARING THE RESULTS

Now that your discussion is finished and you have completed your evaluation, share the results with your group as follows:

1. Ask your group's *observer* to share his or her observations with you. As the observer notes the roles you played in the group, compare these with your self evaluation.

2. Then, ask the *recorder* to share his or her notes of the group's discussion.

3. Finally, take a few minutes to talk over these questions:

   ***What was good and helpful in the group's discussion?

   ***What was there in your discussion that could be improved? In what ways?

MAKING SENSE OF THE RESULTS

Use this discussion as a way to learn about the roles you often play in a discussion and the ways in which you can gain more from discussions.

When the observer shares her or his observation of you, compare it with your own evaluation of yourself. If you disagree, don't argue. Instead, ask the observer about the specifics of what she or he saw. Think about why the observer saw what he or she did.

When you talk about your discussion as a whole, think about what there was in the discussion that was helpful and involving. What needed improvement? Then, share your ideas with your group.

The more you can participate in class discussions in an active and considerate way, the more you will enjoy them. And the more you will learn. Another benefit from participation is that you'll get to know the people in your classes better!

PREPARING FOR DISCUSSIONS

A last word about class discussions: take the time to prepare! You can only participate actively and intelligently if you know something about your topic. For example, if you're going to discuss three articles in your next geology class, be sure to read the articles first.

UNIT X SUMMARY: GAINING FROM DISCUSSIONS

Class discussions give students an opportunity to express, explore, test, and share ideas, understandings, opinions, and questions. *Good* discussions can help you learn, and they can be enjoyable.

Good discussions require:

1. Participants who discuss actively, listen well, and contribute a fair share without dominating or withdrawing

2. A topic for discussion, and ideas, information, theories, feelings, and questions relating to that topic

Ways in which people contribute to the effectiveness of a discussion include:

participating actively

listening carefully and actively

encouraging others

questioning

adding information, ideas, and opinions

clarifying

summarizing

compromising and peacemaking

When you can, try to be prepared for class discussions, so that you'll have more to contribute and more to gain.

LEARNING STUDY SKILLS ON YOUR OWN: X

Dialogue With Yourself

We often assume that discussion requires two people or more. Yet all of us carry on discussions or dialogues with ourselves many times each day. In fact, our internal dialogue is ongoing. Some people talk with themselves only in thoughts. Others use both thought and speech.

In *Learning Study Skills On Your Own* in Unit VIII, you observed your own inner dialogue without directing it. Reflect for a few moments on what you learned through that observation.

You can choose to become more aware of your internal dialogue, your own discussions with yourself. And you can direct these inner discussions to help you learn. For example, when you read, discuss the reading with yourself. Ask yourself questions and answer them. What about X? What does it mean to you? Do you agree or disagree? In what ways? What's important for you to know here? And how would you communicate that to someone else?

UNIT XI: LEARNING FROM VISUALS

WHAT IS A PICTURE WORTH?

"A picture is worth a thousand words." You've undoubtedly heard this statement many times before. Do you think it's true?

If you think it is true, draw a picture below which illustrates its truth. Don't worry about how "good" or artistic the picture is. Just sketch it out quickly. Be prepared to explain your picture.

If you think the statement is false, explain why. Write your explanation in the space below.

THE VALUE OF VISUALS

Even if pictures or visuals are not each worth a thousand words, they can quickly convey a great deal of information. Cartoons, maps, graphs, charts, and pictures are all very effective at communicating concepts, relationships, and details. In a well designed book or article, the visuals both add to and enhance the message of the text.

But you can only find the ideas and information contained within any visual when you choose to examine it carefully.

In this unit, you'll work with several kinds of visuals. You will look for their meanings by using two skills with which you have already worked earlier in this Program:

1. finding a main idea and supporting details
2. asking and answering exploratory questions

TIME LINE

The main idea of any visual is most often indicated by its caption or title. The details are the factual information pictured.

Time lines show when events occurred and the relationships between events in terms of time. Once you've completed the time line in Practice 1, note how quickly your eye and mind pick up the pertinent information, in clear order and in an easily remembered form.

Practice 1: Mark the information below on the time line at the bottom of the page. Then, write a title for this time line.

    1917–1918 — World War I
    1941–1945 — World War II
    1950–1953 — Korean War
    1961–1973 — War in Vietnam

Title: _____

| |
1900   1950   2000

GRAPH

When data has two dimensions, it can be represented by a graph. Graphs clearly and effectively convey a sense of comparison and contrast.

Practice 2: On page 49 in Unit VI, you'll find a paragraph which describes the sharp rise in industrial output during the 18th century in England. Using the graph paper below, draw a graph which shows the growth in the amount of raw cotton imported between 1700 and 1800. Give your graph a title, and then answer the question at the bottom of the page.

Title: _____

What is the main conclusion that you draw from looking carefully at your graph?

_____

_____

_____

ASKING EXPLORATORY QUESTIONS

As you recall from Unit V, *exploratory questions* are questions which go beyond what is stated literally. They involve analysis, implications, critical and creative thinking, and discovery.

Looking at the time line on page 98, an exploratory question you might ask is: given our past experience, is it likely that we will have another war soon? In this case, the visual sets you thinking, but it does not answer the exploratory question.

Practice 3: Look at the time line again, and ask an exploratory question which the time line provokes. Write your question on the lines below.

_____

_____

_____

USING VISUAL AND TEXT TOGETHER

Below you see a computer graphic illustrating the U.S. population density in 1970. Recall that in Unit VI you read an article about computer graphics. Had the visual below been included with that article, you probably would have understood the concept of three dimensional graphics more easily.

Now, turn to pages 55–56, and either skim the article or examine your notes about it. Note that when you examine visuals in the context of a book or article, the visual and the text complement each other, that is, each helps to explain and clarify the other.

U.S. Population Density, 1970, as drawn by a computer.

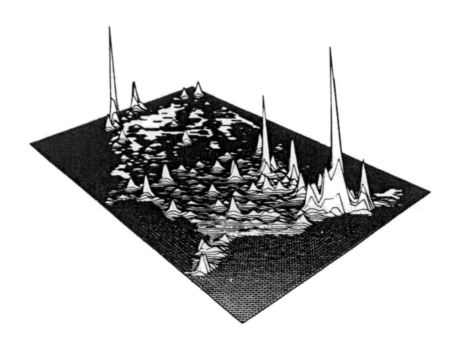

Practice 4: Ask two exploratory questions that are related to the computer graphic about population density. Write your questions on the lines below.

1. _____

_____

2. _____

_____

ASKING QUESTIONS ABOUT VISUALS AND TEXT

One way to ask questions is to organize them around the patterns of organization you learned in Units I and VIII. These patterns include:

description/narration	definition
cause/effect	list
comparison/contrast	sequence/time

When you frame exploratory questions, these patterns can help you get at what is most important. For example, questions of cause and effect usually direct you towards learning about how things are related to each other. And relationships between things are often what you'll find most interesting and important.

Another kind of exploratory question has to do with evaluation. Questions of evaluation require you to judge the accuracy, worth, or value of something. For example, to evaluate a picture or a piece of writing, ask yourself if the author or artist:

1) portrayed the facts accurately

2) interpreted them logically and meaningfully

3) clarified distinctions between fact and opinion

A third type of exploratory question involves appreciation. Questions of this sort ask you to sense how people portrayed in a text or a visual *feel* about what is being shown or described, or to describe how you *feel* as you look at the visual or read the text.

Practice 5: Look at the picture below, and read the text beside it. Then, write questions according to the directions beneath the picture. Although several suggestions are given, just pose one question for each direction.

This cartoon of 1774 depicts the rough treatment Bostonians gave (or wished to give) to tax collectors.

MAIN
IDEA

Ask for a title or a statement of the main idea of the picture.

_____

_____

SUPPORTING
DETAIL

Ask questions about the details of the picture. For example, ask about the positions of the people, the objects in the picture, the way the lines are drawn, etc.

_____

_____

APPRECIATION

Ask questions about the expressions on the people's faces and how the people portrayed in the picture feel. Or, ask how the viewer feels seeing the events in the picture.

_____

_____

SEQUENCE   Ask what happened just before or what led up to this scene in the picture. Ask what events may have followed this scene.

_____

_____

CAUSE/EFFECT   Ask about the causes of the events in this picture, or ask about the effects which might result from this event. Or, ask why certain objects are in the picture, why some of the people are in particular positions, or why people have particular expressions on their faces.

_____

_____

EVALUATION   Ask for a judgment as to the accuracy of the events portrayed in the picture or the clarity of the artist's portrayal.

_____

_____

Practice 6: Visuals are more expensive to print than text, so most book and magazine editors only use visuals that help to convey the main ideas. When you read an article or book, you can learn effectively by using the visuals with the text.

One way to use visuals and text together is shown in steps 1–3 below. Follow these steps as you read the article on pages 105–106.

STEP 1: *Survey* the map on page 105 and the article on page 106. Find the main idea and any supporting details which stand out.

STEP 2: Read the article and take notes in the space below.

STEP 3: Write two exploratory questions on the lines below. Share your questions with your partner(s), and discuss them.

1. _____

_____

2. _____

_____

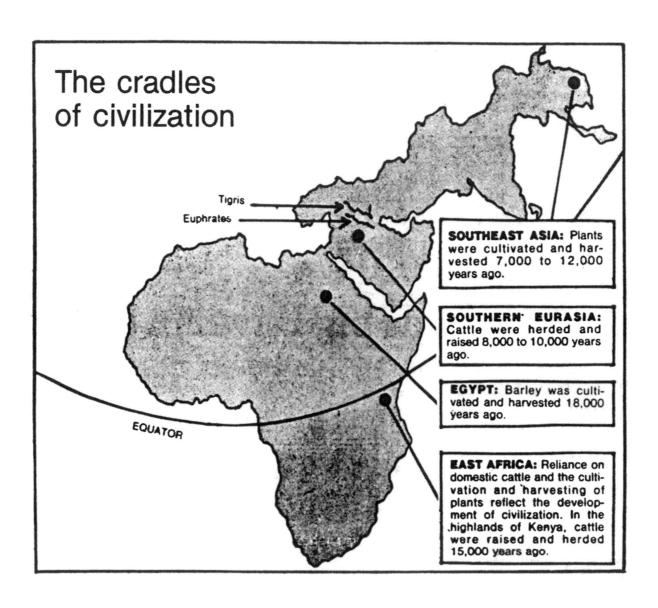

The cradles of civilization

Tigris
Euphrates

EQUATOR

SOUTHEAST ASIA: Plants were cultivated and harvested 7,000 to 12,000 years ago.

SOUTHERN EURASIA: Cattle were herded and raised 8,000 to 10,000 years ago.

EGYPT: Barley was cultivated and harvested 18,000 years ago.

EAST AFRICA: Reliance on domestic cattle and the cultivation and harvesting of plants reflect the development of civilization. In the highlands of Kenya, cattle were raised and herded 15,000 years ago.

Use of cattle 15,000 years ago challenges a theory

by Alan P. Henry

One conventional notion holds that the roots of Western civilization were formed in the Tigris and Euphrates River valleys in the Middle East.

That theory is currently under heavy scientific attack. At least four discoveries have been made in the last decade which suggest many of the elements necessary to the development of Western civilization originated outside the valleys — modern-day Iraq — and were imported to the Near East through trade and cultural diffusion.

The latest evidence challenging the cradle of civilization theory was presented yesterday by UMass anthropologist Dr. Charles Nelson, whose research team found that humans were herding and raising cattle in the highlands of Kenya 15,000 years ago.

The discovery pushes back the age of the earliest known domestic animals 8,000 years. That suggests that the Kenyan settlers contributed to the portion of the mix which would later evolve into a civilization in the Tigris and Euphrates River valleys. Many modern day schoolbooks say plants and animals were first cultivated and domesticated in that river valley 7,000 to 8,000 years ago.

After the control of fire, cultivation of crops and domestication of animals were the most significant events in the development of civilization, anthropologists say. Cultivation of crops provided a dependable, unending source of food, while the domestication of animals provided a steady supply of meat and labor.

Nelson's discoveries are not the first to challenge the conventional Tigris and Euphrates cradle land theory.

Last year, anthropologist Fred Wendorf discovered signs that barley was cultivated and harvested in the Nile River valley (near what is now the Aswan dam) 18,000 years ago.

Researchers in southern Eurasia are finding traces of domesticated cattle also more than 8,000 years ago.

Ten years ago, scientists in southeast Asia found domestic plants between 12,000 and 7,000 years old.

What this means, said Nelson, is that the Tigris and Euphrates cannot technically be called a "cradle" of civilization, since many of its components were not "born" there. "I would call it more of a hub," he said.

"A larger pattern is developing. We can't view what was going on in the Middle East as an isolated event."

"But the evidence our team has unearthed in East Africa, when coupled with recent discoveries from North Africa and Southern Eurasia, suggests that many of the elements necessary to the development of civilization in the Near East actually originated in surrounding areas and were subsequently introduced to the Near East through trade and cultural diffusion," he said.

The age of Nelson's new discoveries was determined using radio carbon and obsidian hydration dating techniques. He called those results "conservative."

That evidence, recovered during a five year excavation program, includes numerous bones and teeth of domestic cattle and a variety of hunted animals, thousands of associated stone and bone artifacts and pottery which may date as early as 10,000 years ago.

The earliest use of domestic cattle, which were herded rather than hunted, took place in the context of local hunting and gathering societies, according to Nelson.

"We did not expect to find the oldest domestic animals in the world," Nelson said yesterday. "We expected they were first in East Africa 3,500 to 4,500 years ago, having come from the Nile Valley and the Egyptian civilization."

Nelson said he expects there will be "healthy skepticism" from some members of the scientific community.

One possible avenue for criticism could be by anyone suggesting that cattle were wild, rather than domestic, Nelson said.

He said he would discount that theory for several reasons. First, there is no known finding or fossil record of wild cattle in the sub-Sahara. Second, wild cattle are not immune or resistant to sleeping sickness and could not have survived in that area because it is surrounded by flies that carry sleeping sickness.

Nelson said the discovery will enable scientists to study the long term skeletal and genetic evolution of cattle under domestic conditions for the first time. The study may also lead to the reassessment of early cattle remains associated with ancient cultures in other parts of the world, he said.

VISUALS AND LEARNING STYLE

You don't need to be an artist to learn from visuals. Nor do you need to be able to visualize clearly, that is, see mental pictures. Almost anyone who pays attention to pictures, charts, and other visuals can learn a good deal from them.

A few other ways of using visuals are:

1. Whenever you find visuals with a reading, survey the visuals first, asking questions about them. After you've finished reading, look at the visuals again and answer your questions.

2. Begin to illustrate your notes whenever you can. If a picture is worth a thousand words (or at least 500), then you can save a lot of writing. Don't worry about artistic quality. Just be sure that you understand what your illustrations mean.

3. Practice seeing visuals in your mind's eye, that is, visualizing them. The more that you practice, the more clearly you'll learn to visualize.

UNIT XI SUMMARY: LEARNING FROM VISUALS

Visuals such as pictures, charts, maps, graphs, and cartoons are very effective at communicating concepts, relationships, and details. In a text or article, each visual usually conveys one main idea which complements what is expressed in the writing.

You can use visuals to provoke exploratory questions. When you look carefully at a visual, it often sets up questions of this sort in you. And when you answer the exploratory questions, you can learn a great deal.

Interesting and helpful exploratory questions often relate to (1) *patterns of organization*, such as cause/effect, list, definition, sequence/time, description/narration, and comparison/contrast, (2) *evaluation*, and (3) *appreciation*.

In a book or article, the text and visuals are designed to complement each other so that each helps to explain, clarify, and develop the other.

Even if you are not an artist, you can still use visuals to help you learn. And the more that you use them, the more helpful they will become to you.

LEARNING STUDY SKILLS ON YOUR OWN: XI

Visualization As Practice

A classic study of visualization as practice involved three groups of student basketball players, none of whom had ever intentionally used visualization before. Group A practiced making free throws every day for 20 days. Group B practiced only on the first and last days. Group C also practiced only on the first and last days but also spent 20 minutes each day imagining making free throws, that is, visualizing shooting free throws.

Group A members improved their shooting by 24%. Group B did not improve at all. *Group C improved by 23%.*

What this study and others like it show is that you can learn by using your imagination, that is, by practicing through visualization.

How does this practice work?

1. First choose what you want to learn and/or improve. Be specific.

2. If you can, see a mental image of what your goal is, that is, what you hope to accomplish through this practice. Make this image as clear and detailed as you can.

3. Practice regularly, for example, every day for five or ten minutes. Begin each practice by seeing the image of your goal. Then, use your imagination to practice whatever you have chosen to learn.

4. When you visualize, make the images as clear and detailed as possible. Also, involve senses other than just sight. In your imagination, feel, hear, and touch your images.

Visualization does not take the place of *doing* when you want to learn. But it can add a great deal to your learning when you use it together with doing.

You can find much more about the uses of visualization and the imagination in *Seeing With The Mind's Eye* by Mike and Nancy Samuels (New York: Random House, 1975).

UNIT XII: PREPARING FOR AND TAKING EXAMS

INTRODUCTION

This unit will show you a strategy for preparing for and taking exams. It will also introduce you to specific skills for answering different kinds of exam questions.

As you work through this unit, compare the methods included here with ones you've used in the past. Take any or all of these methods that work for you, and use them the next time you prepare for and take an exam.

LONG-TERM PREPARATION

The most effective way to prepare for an exam is to do your assignments regularly and stay up-to-date in the course. A good knowledge of the course material gained from ongoing study will be your best ally in an exam.

A STUDY STRATEGY FOR EXAMS

The strategy which you will learn assumes that you've already done the work you need to do for the course and are ready to study for the exam. It includes five steps:

1. Survey your study problem
2. Organize your information
3. Work with your information and learn it
4. Take the exam
5. Learn from the results

You've already selected a course which you're actually taking now with which to work during this unit. As this strategy for study is presented, each step is followed by a practice. *Do each practice using the material (a textbook and other books, notes, etc.) from the course you've chosen.* While you can't get through all of each step in the class time available, you will have a chance to do some of each. Then, you can use what you've learned the next time you need to study for an exam.

I. **SURVEY YOUR STUDY PROBLEM**

Survey your study problem for a course by asking and answering the questions below before you begin to study for an exam. The answers to these questions will help you plan what to study.

A. *What do I need to know for this exam?*

As best you can, find out *what* is likely to be on the exam, and what kinds of questions you may be asked. Do this by asking the instructor, looking at your notes to see what was stressed, and asking students who took the same course with the same instructor previously. Also, some college libraries keep old exams. See if your library or any other college office has old exams given for this course by your instructor.

This seems obvious, but it's worth repeating: don't study what probably won't be on the exam.

B. *Of what I think is likely to be on the exam, what do I already know?*

When you already know part of what you think is likely to be on the exam, just quickly review it in general. Don't study in detail something you already know.

C. *Of what is likely to be on the exam, what don't I already know?*

This is the material on which you want to spend your study time.

D. *How much time do I have to study?*

Divide your available time among your courses. Make a study schedule and use it. Start your studying early enough so you have adequate time for each course.

Practice 1: Imagine that you are about to begin studying for an exam in the course you've chosen. Read questions A–C below carefully, and answer them.

A. What are the main topics and the major skills about which you need to know for this exam? Consider the circled sources of information to the left of the page as you answer.

(from lecture notes)

(from films and tapes)

(from hand-outs)

(from charts and maps)

(from reading notes)

(from labs)

(from ???)

_____

_____

_____

_____

_____

_____

_____

_____

_____

B. Of what you've listed to answer question A, what do you already know? Circle the parts in your answer above that you already know.

C. Now, every part of your answer above which is not circled is a topic or area of information that you don't know well. On the lines below, briefly describe what you would do next if you were preparing for an exam in this course and using your own study method.

_____

_____

_____

_____

_____

II. ORGANIZE YOUR INFORMATION

Once you've figured out what you need to study, the next step is to organize your information. What this involves is deciding what the most important information is from your notes, books, and so on, and then organizing it to make it easier to work with and learn.

You'll also learn a good deal as you organize.

Below you'll find four different ways of organizing information. Depending on the content and format of the exam, you'll want to use some or all of them.

A. Write important *terms* on one side of a 3x5 card. Write the definition on the opposite side. You can use these cards to help you learn the terms you've listed.

B. Write *rules* and *facts* on a 3x5 card. Write the topic or question on the front of the card and the rule or fact on the back. You can use these cards to help you learn the rules or facts.

C. Diagram, map, chart, or graph information that's important so you can easily see relationships. Gather as much information as you can into a series of diagrams, maps, charts, graphs, etc.

D. Use a *question outline* or *question map* to organize your studying.

Outline or map your course on 2–3 pages of paper. Phrase each outline or map topic as a question. Be sure to include questions about information such as:

1. Laws, rules, terms, definitions
2. Important generalizations and concepts, and details to support them
3. Important skills you need to have mastered
4. Information from audio-visual sources
5. Material your instructor says will be on the exam

As you develop your question outline or map, keep related concepts and areas of information together. Use your course syllabus to help you organize. For example, if a film related to an early part of the course is shown later in the semester, integrate the question(s) about the film with the material to which it relates. (If you expect to do a lot of re-ordering, you may want to write your questions initially on separate 3x5 cards. Then, once you've organized them, transfer the questions to an outline or map.)

Try to include in your outline or map all of the topics that you expect to be on the exam.

When you've completed your question outline or map, you can use it as a primary tool in studying for the exam. Ways to use it will be described in the next section of this unit.

Practice 2: In the space below, create a *question map* or *outline* for *part* of the course for which you are preparing for an imaginary exam. Do only as much as you can finish in *10 minutes.*

III. WORK WITH YOUR INFORMATION AND LEARN IT

Now, you've "psyched out" the exam, that is, figured out what is likely to be on it. And you've taken that information and organized it for efficient study.

The next step is to work with the material and learn it. Below you'll find many suggestions for how you can do this. (You may also want to review Unit VIII in this book, "Understanding And Improving Your Memory," and use some of the suggestions there.)

A. Use your question outline or map by asking yourself the questions and rehearsing the answers in your mind, aloud, on paper, and in discussion. When you don't know the answers, look them up in your notes, books, etc. You may want to jot them down on your outline or map. (If you're not certain about your answers, be sure to check them. You don't want to learn incorrect information.)

B. Work with one section of your question outline or map at a time. When you answer the questions, be sure to support generalizations and main ideas with important details.

C. Study any 3x5 cards and maps, charts, graphs, and diagrams that you've made as their information fits into your question outline or map.

D. After you study each section of your question outline or map, review where it fits in the course as a whole.

E. If you work with a friend or a study group, you can design one question outline or map together. Then, have each person be responsible for teaching one part of it to the rest of the group members.

F. As you study and learn, alone or with others, reinforce your memory in any of the following ways:

   1. Repeat the same information and ideas in different words.

   2. Relate less important ideas to more important ideas.

   3. Relate the information you are trying to learn to what you already know about the subject.

   4. Criticize the material. Evaluate it and discuss it. Be sure to support your criticism with facts, ideas, details, etc.

   5. Imagine that you are teaching the material to a younger or less knowledgeable student. Actually present the material for this purpose.

   6. Use mental images or draw pictures to illustrate important concepts and processes.

   7. Use mnemonics when you can. (Look at Unit VIII to find a discussion of what mnemonics are.)

G. Practice any skills which you will need to use competently on the exam, for example, solving problems or using statistics.

Finally, think about what kinds of test questions you are likely to encounter on the exam. Go over the information you gathered in step #1 about the kinds of questions to expect. Consider any particular ways that you can prepare for specific kinds of questions. For example, if you know you will have to write an essay about one topic which you will choose from several options, you might be able to prepare the essay in your mind ahead of time.

In the next section of this unit, you'll find suggested skills you can learn and use to help you answer the most common kinds of test questions.

DON'T FEEL OVERWHELMED by all the suggestions you've just read. You don't need to use them all at once. Learn a few at a time and see how they help you. Then, you can come back and learn a few more.

113

Practice 3: Take the question outline or map which you created for Practice 2, and use it to study. Try at least 2 of the suggestions described above. You can try more.

You'll have 10 minutes to study. At the end of that time, briefly evaluate 2 of the suggestions you used on the lines below. What was helpful about each method? What wasn't so helpful?

SUGGESTIONS FOR LEARNING	EVALUATION
1. _____ _____	_____ _____ _____ _____ _____
2. _____ _____	_____ _____ _____ _____ _____

IV. TAKE THE EXAM

Below you'll find many suggestions for how to take an exam. You've probably heard many of these before. You may use some. Others you may have chosen to disregard.

As you read them now, try to consider them anew from the point of view described in the paragraphs below.

What is an exam? An exam is an opportunity, usually a required one, for you to communicate what you know and understand about a subject. Most often you do this within a framework dictated by your instructor.

The more you know about (1) how the exam works and (2) what's important from your instructor's viewpoint, the more effectively you can communicate what you do know.

Read the suggestions below. Place a check to the left of any suggestion which you find helpful *and* which you'd use.

Suggestions For Taking An Exam

A. Be physically prepared. Take care of your body, because the condition of your body has a direct effect on your mind. Get a good night's sleep and eat breakfast or lunch before the exam.

B. Be prepared for the exam. Arrive on time, and bring all your materials (pens, pencils, and, if allowed and needed, calculator, notes, dictionary, etc.).

C. When you receive the exam, first survey it. Get a sense of the whole. (If important information comes to mind while you are surveying the exam, jot it down next to the question, so you can refer to it when you need it.)

D. Quickly plan your time use for the exam. Allow more time for questions which:

    1. Carry a high point value

    2. Are longer; for example, essays

    3. Are less familiar to you in terms of content and/or format

E. Start with the questions you find easiest to answer, because they tend to build your confidence. You can probably answer them quickly. And they may make the harder questions easier for you by reminding you of information you can use in later answers. Keep in mind that the questions at the end of the test may be easier for you.

F. Read the directions for each section of the test carefully as you work along.

G. If you are asked for more than one type of information in a question, number each type you must include in your answer.

        #1   #2

EXAMPLE: Explain the causes of the Revolutionary War. Tell which cause was most important and why.
       #3

H. Give the most direct answer you can within the terms stated by the test. For example, if the question says *list,* just list your answer; you don't need to write it in sentences.

I. When a question includes more than one part, be sure to answer all of the different parts.

J. Answer all questions on an exam, unless there is a penalty for guessing. Even if there is such a penalty, if you can eliminate a couple of choices and guess from two or three, go ahead and do so. The odds are then that you'll gain more than you'll lose.

K. When you want to skip a question and return to it, place a star or check in the margin to the left of the question to remind you.

L. While you take an exam, try to isolate yourself from distractions in the testing room. Try not to pay attention to or worry about what other people are doing. Just keep yourself focused on what you need to do.

M. When you have the time, check over your answers.

Practice 4: Look over the suggestions that you checked above. Choose the three which you feel would be most valuable for you to learn and use. Jot them down on the lines below.

1. _____

2. _____

3. _____

V. LEARN FROM THE RESULTS

The last step in this strategy is to use the results of the exam for learning. Be sure you get your exam back, answers and questions, and then:

    A. Go over your incorrect answers, and find out why you missed each item.

        1. Did you not know the information? Do you know why you didn't know?

        2. Did you not follow or understand the instructions? Do you know why?

    B. Next, quickly go over all of the items on the exam, placing a check next to each one that you correctly predicted. Did you predict 50% or more? If so, you did well. If not, how can you do better next time?

    C. Reflect on your successes and your errors on the exam. Ask yourself: how can I better prepare myself next time?

COMMON TYPES OF EXAM QUESTIONS

There are four common types of exam questions which instructors use at the college level: short answer, essay, multiple choice, and problem. The activities in this section include all four.

SHORT ANSWER QUESTIONS

This type of test question has two common formats: (1) fill-in-the-blanks, and (2) *define, identify, list,* etc. Both types usually require the knowledge of vocabulary, terms, laws, etc. Often this is the kind of information you would put on 3x5 cards.

For these questions, try to give an answer even when you're not certain of your information. Some instructors give credit for ideas stated in terms other than the ones intended. Others give partial credit if you indicate some knowledge.

Practice 5: Imagine that you are writing exam questions for the same course with which you've been working throughout this unit. Write one short answer question for each direction below.

Then, answer your questions. Or, switch books and answer your partner's questions. Then, go over the answers with your partner(s).

A. Write a fill-in-the-blank question.

QUESTION: _____

_____

_____

B. *Define* means clearly state the meaning, usually without examples. Write a question which begins with "define."

QUESTION: _____

ANSWER: _____

_____

C. *Identify* means briefly present facts about something or somebody which tell what or who the thing or person is. Write a question which begins with "identify."

QUESTION: _____

ANSWER: _____

_____

D. *List* or *enumerate* means write a series of facts, names, etc. Write a question which begins with "list" or "enumerate."

QUESTION: _____

ANSWER: _____

_____

ESSAY QUESTIONS

Many students find essay questions the most difficult. Yet essay questions often give you the best opportunity on an exam to *choose* what you will answer and show what you have learned. This is true because (1) your instructor will often ask you to answer only one or two questions of several given, and because (2) it's up to you to organize and develop your essays in ways that make sense to you.

Answering essay questions becomes easier when you work with a plan or strategy. Below you see the outline of such a plan. In this section, you'll learn about this plan or strategy in more detail and practice parts of it.

If you don't have your own strategy for answering essay questions, try the one here. If you already have your own, examine the one here and see if you want to adopt any parts of it.

A PLAN FOR ANSWERING ESSAY QUESTIONS

1. If you have a choice, choose the question(s) you will answer.
2. Read the question carefully. Be sure you understand it.
3. Rephrase the question as a topic sentence.
4. Think about what you want to say. Then, briefly outline or map your answer.
5. Write the essay, using your outline or map as a guide.
6. If you have time, read over your essay. Make any desired changes.

1. **IF YOU HAVE A CHOICE, CHOOSE THE QUESTION(S) YOU WILL ANSWER.**

   If you have a choice of questions, read all of the possibilities. Select the one(s) which (1) you know most about and (2) which you can develop effectively in the time available.

2. **READ THE QUESTION CAREFULLY. BE SURE YOU UNDERSTAND IT.**

   One key to understanding essay questions is understanding the words instructors use to ask these questions. In Practice 6 below, you'll learn or review some terms commonly used to ask essay questions.

Practice 6: On a piece of scratch paper, write definitions or explanations for the two words below which your instructor assigns to you. When everyone in the class is ready, you'll discuss the definitions for all of the words below, polish them, and then write them in the appropriate spaces to form a glossary of essay question terms.

analyze: _____

compare: _____

contrast: _____

describe: _____

discuss: _____

evaluate/criticize: _____

_____

explain: _____

outline: _____

summarize: _____

trace (or "trace the development of") _____

_____

Practice 7: On the lines below, write one good essay question which could be on the final exam for the same course with which you've worked throughout this unit.

_____

_____

_____

3. **REPHRASE THE QUESTION AS A TOPIC SENTENCE.**

Often you can take the question itself and rephrase it to serve as the topic sentence of the first paragraph in your essay. This helps you make sure that you're on the right track with your answer. It also tells your instructor that you understand the question and intend to answer it directly.

Practice 8: On the lines below, rephrase the question you wrote for Practice 7 as a topic sentence for the first paragraph of your essay. Or, copy your partner's question on the lines below marked "Partner's Question." Then, rephrase it as a topic sentence.

ESSAY QUESTION REPHRASED AS A TOPIC SENTENCE

_____

_____

_____

_____

PARTNER'S QUESTION

_____

_____

_____

_____

4. **THINK ABOUT WHAT YOU WANT TO SAY. THEN, BRIEFLY OUTLINE OR MAP YOUR ANSWER.**

Before you start to outline or map, take a little time to think about what you intend to say. Some essay questions ask you mostly to "show all you know" about a topic. Others direct you to develop an argument, an analysis, or a comparison and contrast. Be sure you know what you're trying to do. Then, jot down a *brief* outline or map of your answer.

Don't cross out or discard your outline or map. If you don't finish writing your essay in time, hand in your outline or map as proof of what you know about the topic, and ask your instructor for partial credit.

Practice 9: In the space marked "outline or map of essay", write an outline or map for an essay which answers the question you rephrased in Practice 8.

Do the best that you can with this outline or map given what you know now.

OUTLINE OR MAP OF ESSAY

5. WRITE THE ESSAY, USING YOUR OUTLINE OR MAP AS A GUIDE.

As you write the essay, try to be sure that everything you include bears directly on the question. Be direct. Don't wander.

Include an introduction and a conclusion in your essay. One way to think of this is that the introduction says what you're going to show, prove, or explain. Then, the body of the essay does just that. Finally, the conclusion restates in other terms what your essay has accomplished.

Write clear sentences.

Use transitions such as *first, second, most important* etc. as you make your points.

6. **IF YOU HAVE TIME, READ OVER YOUR ESSAY. MAKE ANY DESIRED CHANGES.**

The most important concern at this point is to be sure that you've answered all of the parts of the essay question. If you've omitted a part of the question, at least quickly sketch out an outline or map response to it.

MULTIPLE CHOICE QUESTIONS

Some students favor multiple choice questions because they only have to choose the correct answer. Others find multiple choice questions "tricky" and difficult.

As with other kinds of exam questions, you'll be more successful with multiple choice questions when you know skills and strategies you can use to answer them. Below you'll find a strategy for answering multiple choice questions.

1. First, carefully read the question. Then, even before you look at the options, try to think of the answer. When you know the answer, compare this with the options, and pick the one closest to your answer.

2. When you don't know the answer just from reading the question, then read *all* of the options or choices. As you do this, narrow your choices. Eliminate the ones which are clearly wrong. Pick the best answer from the choices which are still available.

3. Use your common sense. Often, even when you don't really know the right answer, you can figure it out by using some information you do know which relates to it.

4. Here are several specific tips for answering multiple choice questions:

    a. Watch out for specific determiners such as *always, all, none,* and *never.* They usually mean the option is incorrect.

    b. Watch out for options such as *all of the above* and *none of the above.* Sometimes they are correct.

    c. Over-long and over-short options tend to be correct.

    d. General statements and ones which are qualified by words *generally, often, mostly,* etc. tend to be correct.

Practice 10: Write two multiple choice questions which could be on the final exam for the course with which you've worked throughout this unit. Try to make at least one of these questions "tricky."

Exchange books with your partner when you have finished writing your questions. Then, answer your partner's questions. When you are both ready, go over all of the questions.

1. _____
   _____
   _____
   _____

2. _____
   _____
   _____
   _____

PROBLEMS

Exams in math and science courses often include problems. Solving problems of this kind is beyond the scope of this unit except for a few general hints listed below.

1. Read the problem carefully to find out what you are being asked.

2. Read through it again to find the information you need to solve the problem.

3. Organize the information in whatever way(s) helps you to solve the problem. This may include graphs, charts, diagrams, maps, pictures, etc.

4. Solve the problem.

5. Check your answer with common sense and, if possible, estimation. Does it make sense? Is it "in the ball park"?

A FINAL WORD: "TESTWISENESS"

Understanding how test or exam questions work is called "testwiseness," that is, being wise about the test. An analogy you can use to help you understand this is to see the test or exam as a game. Being "testwise" means, then, that you know and understand the rules of the game.

When you are "testwise," you can take what you know about a subject and communicate effectively to your instructor through the particular questions on a test. "Testwiseness" doesn't take the place of studying for an exam. Rather, what it does is help you take what you've learned through your studying and make sure that you can convey it clearly on the exam.

If you want to learn more about taking tests, two helpful resources are:

Millman, Jason and Walter Pauk. *How to Take Tests.* New York: McGraw-Hill Book Co., 1969.

Feder, Bernard. *The Complete Guide to Taking Tests.* Englewood Cliffs, New Jersey: Prentice-Hall, Inc., 1979.

UNIT XII SUMMARY: PREPARING FOR AND TAKING EXAMS

When you study for exams, use a strategy like the one below.

1. **Survey your study problem**

   Ask yourself and then answer the following questions:

   A. What do I need to know for this exam?

   B. Of what I think is likely to be on the exam, what do I already know?

   C. Of what is likely to be on the exam, what don't I already know?

   D. How much time do I have to study?

2. **Organize your information**

   Decide what the most important information is from your notes, books, etc., and organize it to make it easier to work with and learn. Write important terms, rules, and facts on 3x5 cards. Diagram, map, chart, or graph information so you can easily see relationships. Create a *question outline* or *question map* to help you organize your studying.

3. **Work with your information and learn it**

   Use your question outline or map by asking yourself the questions and rehearsing your answers. Study your maps, graphs, charts, diagrams, and 3x5 cards. Reinforce your memory by restating information in different words, explaining ideas and concepts to someone else, evaluating and criticizing material, and using mental images or drawing pictures to illustrate important concepts. Practice any skills that you'll need to use on the exam. Finally, think about what kinds of test questions you expect to encounter on the exam, and prepare for them in any way that you can.

4. **Take the exam**

   Be physically prepared. When you receive the exam, survey it, and plan your time use for answering the questions. Read the directions carefully. Give the most direct answer you can. Be sure to answer all questions, unless there's a penalty for guessing. While you take the exam, keep yourself focused on what you need to do. Don't let yourself be distracted by others.

5. **Learn from the results**

   When you get your exam back, go over it. Find out why you missed each item that you answered incorrectly. Evaluate how many questions on the exam you accurately predicted. Reflect on your successes and errors on the exam.

There are four common types of exam questions which instructors use at the college level.

1. **Short answer questions**

   These are usually (1) fill-in-the-blanks, and (2) define, identify, list, etc. Both types often require the knowledge of vocabulary, terms, laws, and facts.

2. **Essay questions**

   A. If you have a choice, choose the question(s) you will answer.

   B. Read the question carefully. Be sure you understand it.

   C. Rephrase the question as a topic sentence.

   D. Think about what you want to say. Then, briefly outline or map your answer.

   E. Write the essay, using your outline or map as a guide.

   F. If you have time, read over your essay. Make any desired changes.

3. **Multiple choice questions**

   A. First, read the question carefully. Try to think of an answer before you look at the options. When you know the answer, compare this with the options, and pick the best one.

   B. When you don't know the answer, read all of the options carefully. Eliminate the choices which are clearly wrong. Pick the best answer from the choices which are still available.

   C. Use your common sense. Even when you don't really know the right answer, you can often figure it out.

4. **Problems**

   (A) Read the problem carefully to find out what you are being asked. (B) Read through the problem again to find the information you need. (C) Organize the information in whatever way(s) helps you to solve the problem. (D) Solve the problem. (E) Check your answer with common sense and, if possible, with estimation.

   Understanding how test or exam questions work is called "testwiseness," that is, being wise about the test. The more "testwise" you are, the better you'll be able to communicate effectively to your instructor through the particular questions on a test.

LEARNING STUDY SKILLS ON YOUR OWN: XII

Relaxation and Test Anxiety

Sometimes you may feel anxious or nervous before or during an exam. Some anxiety or nervousness is a very natural feeling. Most people feel this way at times. But too much anxiety can interfere with your performance on a test or exam. When you feel that test anxiety is getting in your way as you prepare for and take a test, what can you do?

One way to lessen test anxiety is to become "testwise." Studies have shown that students who understand how test questions work and are skilled in answering these questions tend to feel less anxious or nervous about exams. The more that you feel that you understand and are prepared for a test, the less nervous you'll be about it. The more capable you know you are as a test taker, the more confident you'll feel during tests.

Another way to lessen test anxiety is to learn to *relax*. The ability to relax and focus your attention on the test is a very helpful tool. One method for relaxing is the exercise described below. Read the directions a few times, and then try it. Once you've learned to relax in this way, you'll probably find many uses for this skill.

RELAXATION EXERCISE

Sit in a comfortable position with your spine straight.

Close your eyes, and take a couple of smooth, deep breaths. Feel the air come in all the way down into your abdomen, then feel the air go out again.

Now, sit quietly and just be aware of your breathing for a little while. Don't consciously try to control it. Just be aware of your breath coming in, your breath going out.

Now, with your inner eye, imagine a peaceful scene that you appreciate and enjoy. See this peaceful scene as clearly as you can. Involve all of your senses. What do you see? Hear? Smell? Feel? Make this scene very peaceful.

Do you see yourself in your peaceful scene? If you're not already there, put yourself there if you can. And feel the relaxation of this peaceful, calm place. Feel yourself very relaxed, and very wide awake and alert.

Now, with your inner voice, tell yourself: I am relaxed and alert and ready to begin. I am relaxed and alert and ready to begin. Say this two or three times more.

Now, gently open your eyes. You're ready to begin the exam.

123

A Few Notes About Relaxation

If you practice the exercise above, you can learn to relax easily and quickly. Read the suggestions below, and then try the exercise again.

1. There is no *right* or *wrong* way to relax. The method you've just practiced is one that works well for many people. Feel free to change it in any way that makes it feel better for you.

2. If you don't see mental pictures or images clearly, don't allow that to stand in your way. You don't need to see mental pictures to relax. Instead, be aware of your breathing for a longer time. Follow your breath coming in and going out. Then, tell yourself: "I am relaxed and alert and ready to begin." Repeat this four or five times before you open your eyes.

3. When you relax, be sure to stay awake and alert. It's not hard to do this when you try. If you relax but don't stay alert, you might get sleepy. And that won't help.

4. You can use relaxation both when you study for a test and when you take the test. Once you've learned how to relax, it only takes a minute and can help you become calm and clear and focused.

Breinigsville, PA USA
08 September 2010
245001BV00005B/1/P